IN THE MIDST OF

CHAOS

HOME IS THE MOST DANGEROUS PLACE TO BE

Created by

Mildred D. Muhammad

Published by The Book Chief Publishing House 2022

Suite 2A, Blackthorn House, St Paul's Square, Birmingham, B3 1RL

www.thebookchief.com

Book Cover Design: Deearo Marketing

Editor: Laura Billingham

Typesetting / Formatting / Publishing: Sharon Brown

THE BOOK CHIEF®

IGNITE YOUR WRITING

Table of Contents

Foreword

By Dr. Denise C. McCain

Director, Prince George's County Family Justice Center

Gender Based Violence Researcher

With more than 30 years in the field as a grassroots advocate domestic violence program administrator and visionary thought leader, I have had the unique opportunity to work with thousands of survivors of intimate partner violence, many of whom were typically living in the midst of chaos, hurt, and pain that is commonly experienced as a victim of domestic abuse and violence.

It takes an inordinate amount of strength and courage for a victim to speak out and ask for help. However, far too often they are re-victimized by the very systems that were designed to protect them, or they are blamed, shamed, or simply not believed, which is why the vast majority never report their abuse and sadly make the choice to suffer in silence.

Similar such circumstances led to my initial introduction to Mildred Muhammad. That was nearly twenty years ago during what was a most tumultuous time in her life, as she was experiencing her own very personal storm and struggle to reclaim her life in the aftermath of abuse. Like the women in this book, Mildred Muhammad epitomizes the definition of 'survivor'. She is a powerful voice in the movement to combat gender based violence and deserves great acclaim for her ongoing efforts to empower, educate and uplift those who are impacted by intimate partner abuse. Today, I am proud to call her a colleague, friend and fierce advocate!

"In the Midst of Chaos' is an important and critical commentary on the generally misunderstood dynamic of domestic violence as conveyed by those who have actually experienced and survived their abuse. The stories are raw, emotional, and profoundly eye-opening. This book skilfully pulls back the curtain on the oftentimes hidden and shamefully concealed atrocities of domestic violence that victims experience at the hands of those who profess to love them. The harrowing stories as told by these courageous survivors are difficult to read, while at the same time, hard to turn away from.

This book is a must read for survivors, many of whom have given up, lost hope and just don't see a way out. If this speaks to you, I implore you to let the voices of these survivors serve as a testament of hope and confirmation that your tomorrow can and will be better than today, even if you can't see it... that's called FAITH!

It is equally important that criminal justice officials, judiciary, clergy, and community at large read this book as it effectively dispels myths and erroneous assumptions about victims of intimate partner violence. Specifically, who they are, how they get into abusive relationships, and the misdirected question about 'why they stay', but more appropriately, what it takes for them to leave and remain safe. No one wants, consciously chooses, or most importantly, deserves to be abused. Anyone can become a victim of intimate partner violence.

As evident in the stories of these survivors, domestic violence is a pernicious societal ill that obscures hope and arrests dreams of tomorrow for its victims, but know that there is life after abuse!

Introduction

I am Mildred D. Muhammad, and the ex-wife of the DC Sniper (John A Muhammad). IN THE MIDST OF CHAOS is a HIGH-PROFILE series of books and events that will highlight the stories and courageous journeys of those who have suffered, endured, and escaped abuse in any form. According to law enforcement, I was his target! Yes, you read that correctly. All those people were killed because John Muhammad wanted to cover his tracks so he could eventually kill me and gain custody of his children. It was a domestic abuse/child custody issue. Although 2022 marks the 20th anniversary of this horrible event, which claimed the lives of 17 people and severely injured another 10, 2022 also marks my 22nd anniversary of my freedom and safety.

This international anthology, "In the Midst of Chaos," the first of three, addresses domestic violence and abuse. Numerous authors have assembled to share their stories and discuss how they struggled to leave violent relationships on their own for years without much help. Their experiences will have you on the edge of your seat as well as how society handles victims who ask for help. We are sharing our experiences to assist others in speaking up in an effort to inspire others to stop suffering in silence. Domestic abuse and violence don't have a race, gender, religion, creed or color. It occurs from the very rich to the very poor of every culture, worldwide. Abuse increases in silent.

The world's cultures have long recognized domestic violence and abuse as a problem that affects individual families. We have seen women and men being assaulted and we have turned our heads away, saying to ourselves or others, "That's not my responsibility." Many women and men attempted coming out and telling people about the abuse happening in their homes, but they were either rejected or made to feel like it was their responsibility. Victims and children in particular are affected by the abuser's instability, as well as the rest of the world. It becomes a problem for the community when a victim seeks assistance somewhere other than at home. The fear of not being believed keeps many domestic abuse victims from speaking up just as much as threats from their abusers. However, some people hold the view that abuse victims don't deserve any sort of assistance because they choose to be abused.

Many people assume that physical violence is always involved when talking about domestic violence and abuse. However, the two are distinct groups, and up to 80% of domestic violence victims never show signs of physical harm like scars or bruises. Domestic abuse encompasses stalking as well as verbal, psychological, spiritual, and financial abuse to name a few.

These abuses law enforcement does not respond or take seriously. After any physical assault, which include, hitting, slapping, mutilation, and even death are all examples of domestic violence.

Even though victim-blaming is an attack on the victim, many individuals still have the most insensitive question to put to them. The question is, "Why do you stay?" Some people think that by asking this question, they would startle the victim into reacting and leaving the relationship. In actuality, by asking this question, you are placing the entire burden of the abusive relationship on the victim, as if leaving will make the abuse stop. On the other hand, up to 75% of victims who attempt to leave an abusive relationship are either harmed or killed. Even when the victim leaves, the abuse continues.

It's time to reframe the way we speak to victims while downplaying the abuser's actions. Taking the responsibility away from the victim and placing it where it belongs is holding the abuser responsible for the chaos, they are wreaking in their family's lives. Start by asking the abuser, "Why do you abuse?"

Keep in mind, every victim wants to leave, but all victims don't know how!

Dedication

In the Midst of Chaos was chosen as the title of this book to reflect the tremendous pressure a victim experiences while attempting to defend themselves and their children while maintaining composure.

The phrase "In the Midst of Chaos" refers to being in the thick of the chaos and maintaining your composure. It is vital to retain even a modest amount of inner calm, although this is difficult to do.

This book is devoted to all victims who endure silent torment, regardless of gender.

We hope that after reading these chapters, you will have the confidence to use strategy when looking for resources, find your voice and use it wisely to speak up, and eventually escape the abusive relationship. You can get in touch with any of us for help. We will do everything we can to assist. Our contact information is provided.

Mildred D. Muhammad

Award Winning Global Keynote
Speaker, Certified Consultant with
the Office for Victims of Crime,
Certified Domestic Violence
Advocate

Chapter 1

SCARED SILENT

By Mildred D. Muhammad

Domestic abuse and violence have progressed from a global epidemic to a global pandemic within a pandemic. The world realized the gravity of the situation when it was reported that more women were killed during the pandemic than soldiers in Desert Storm.

We must change the narrative and stop asking victims, "WHY DO YOU STAY?" Start asking abusers, 'WHY DO YOU ABUSE?' When you ask the victims, 'WHY DO YOU STAY?', you are placing the total responsibility of the abuse on the victim instead of holding the abuser accountable and responsible for terrorizing their family. When victims attempt to escape an abusive relationship, up to 75% of them are either injured or killed.

Since our culture is mainly visual, if other people overlook the injuries, their abuse doesn't occur. 80% of victims lack visible scars that would indicate they are victims. What, then, should they do?

A Different Man Returned

I had been married to John for 12 years. Our family consisted of three children: one son and two daughters.

John served in the Army as an SGT with the 84th Combat Engineers Unit. At the time of Desert Storm, we were stationed in Bindlach, Germany, with our first child. Before Desert Storm, John was the "GO-TO" man for a good time. He was the life of the party, animated and eager to assist anyone. He stayed for three months until he was forced to return due to a shoulder injury.

He was a different man when he returned home.

He was diagnosed with PTSD and had not been debriefed. He was reticent, rocking back and forth when he was seated. I asked him if he was okay. He said I'm good. I wondered whether he wanted to talk about what happened in Saudi. He said you're asking too many questions.

There were times when John's behavior would revert to who he was before Saudi. However, those times were becoming fewer and fewer, to the point where he had become a total stranger. I was constantly taken aback by his actions. He would change just as I thought I knew him again.

Moving

The Bindlach Army base was shut down. John was sent on orders to Ft. Ord, California. In 1992, with two children, we headed back to the States. Our last child was born in 1993. The Army closed Fort Ord, and John was given orders for Ft Lewis, Washington.

John chose to leave the service one year later. We founded Express Car/Truck Mechanic and would operate as a mobile vehicle repair business in Tacoma, Washington. Women with children made up many of our clients. It wasn't long before he began servicing the women too!

John was the only mechanic that worked on our cars. One day my children and I were going to the grocery store, and as I approached the stop sign, I applied the brakes. They didn't work. I pushed the pedal to the floor and then pumped the brakes. That didn't work either. As we entered the main street, I began praying that we would not be hit by cars. Thank God no cars were approaching us. I was able to steer the car to the park. I had a tow truck take it to another shop. That mechanic said somebody doesn't like you. Your brake lines were cut. I'll fix them. He told me to only bring my car to him for repairs. All I could think of was John was trying to kill his children and me.

I asked for a divorce. He stated he didn't want a divorce.

I told him I was trying to give him his freedom so he could be with whomever he wanted and not lie to me. It was when he left that the chaos began.

No physical scars

John moved out but didn't leave the keys to the house behind. He began coming in during the night. I'd hear the key going into the lock, the door opening/closing, as he's walking down the hallway into my bedroom. I opened my eyes, just a little, to watch him walk around one end of my bed to the other. Lean over to listen to me breathe, stand up and walk out of the house. Our baby girl, Taalibah, woke up the third time and heard him. She came into the room and said, Daddy! I sat up in bed. He looked at me, picked up Taalibah, handed her to me and walked away.

I decided to change the locks and told the children. Unannounced, John dropped by to see his children. 'So, big man, what's going on?' he asked of our son. He said, 'Daddy, Mommy is going to have the locks changed.' He asked why I was having the locks changed. I mentioned that my key isn't working. He replied that his key was also not working. Let's go to the front door, he said. He took my key and tried to insert it into the lock. He also tried his key. Both keys were inoperative. He stated, "I'm going to remove the lock and bring back another." A straight pin fell out of the door as he removed the lock. He'd tampered with the lock but didn't seem to see the pin. I did and said nothing. He didn't come back. I propped a chair under the doorknob and sat up with a knife in my hand to secure me, my children and my mom from possible intruders. Three days later, the locksmith arrived and changed the locks.

I noticed my phone wasn't ringing. I picked up the receiver to make sure there was a ringtone, and there was. As soon as I hung up the phone, it rang. It was a friend of ours. She stated she called to check on me. I asked her what number she had called. She said, 'John changed your number and wanted me to call you.' I asked her for my number. She refused to tell me, stating she was afraid of John. She hung up. I called the phone company and had the number changed. As soon as I hung up, the phone rang. It was John. He asked, who told you to change this number? I responded, 'I don't need your permission to change this number'. He said, 'don't change it again.' I called the phone company again. I requested a supervisor. I asked him, 'isn't there a law against changing the number of residents without their consent?' He paused and said 'yes'. I explained to him what was happening. He said he would put a code on my phone so that if he tried again, he would be unable to get my number. John had befriended a woman at the phone company to inform him of when I changed my number. She would give him my new number. However, since the code had been placed on my number, she couldn't give him that one.

John came over again, unannounced, to see his children. I told him he couldn't roll up without calling ahead when he felt like it. He pushed his way into the house. I fell back and hit my head on the fireplace. I got up and called the police, and he ran away. The police came, and I informed them of what had happened. They asked was his name on the lease. I said it was. They told me there was nothing they could do because he had a right to be in the home. However, they asked whether I had a restraining order. I said no. They gave me the paperwork to file at the courthouse. The next day, I went to the courthouse. They gave me one sheet of paper with ten questions. I began crying and asking myself, how did I get here? I called my friend. She told me to complete the paperwork so it would establish a paper trail. I had a court date a few days later. I went back to the courthouse. The judge read my petition and said, you need to get away from this guy. I said, your honor, I'm trying to do that. He gave me a lifetime restraining order. I don't know if they give those out anymore. Sadly, the restraining order included visitation with his children.

I returned home. My brother was there then John arrived unannounced, stating we needed to talk. Because my brother was there, I wasn't afraid. We went into the garage. John said, 'you are not going to raise our children alone. You have become my enemy, and as my enemy, I will kill you.' I didn't want to appear afraid, so I responded, 'well, I've been sleeping with the enemy all this time; what else are you going to do?' He charged at me. I ran to my brother. I told my brother, 'John is going to kill me; he's going to kill me.' He responded, 'John's not going to kill you. He's just playing.' I never went to my brother again for help. Victims are short on time to explain the danger they are in. If you cannot assist, move out of the way so they can find someone who will.

Custodial Interference = Kidnapping

We had to find someone to pick up our children from me and take them back to John for visitation. We decided on a mutual friend that decided to help. The first weekend went well. They were picked up on Friday and returned Sunday afternoon. The second weekend was my mother's birthday, March 27th. She wanted to go to Country Buffet for her birthday meal. I told the friend who picked up the children on Friday to tell John they had to be back by noon so we could take my mom to Country Buffet. He said he would let him know. However, Sunday at noon, the friend showed up with a note from John.

I opened the note, and there were two dollars attached. The message was from our youngest daughter, Taalibah. It read, 'Happy Birthday Grandma'. I looked at the friend and asked, where are my children?' He said you'd have to ask John. I immediately called him, and my son picked up. I said, ask your dad what time you are coming home. He said, Mom, dad said we would be home at 7:30. I asked where they were. He said they were at Walmart getting clothes from a list I'd given his dad. I said, 'Okay.' 7:30 came, and no children. I started blowing up his pager. He called at 11:35 pm, stating they were en route from Seattle and would be there shortly. As I was hanging up the phone, I felt butterflies and thought... something's wrong.

Since it was a Sunday, I thought that perhaps he would take the children to school the next day. I called the school for four days, and they said my children were not there. I finally went there on that Friday. They were not there. I came home and called the police. They said there was nothing they could do since there wasn't a parenting plan. I found out later that he had emptied our bank accounts and informed the landlord that he would not be paying the rent. Others knew where my children were and did not tell me. It would be 18 months before I saw my children again.

The Sniper

After getting my children during emergency custody in September 2001, we went to live with my sister in the DC area, assisting her with the care of our mother. In late September 2002, someone was randomly shooting people. Law enforcement told us to look for two Caucasians in a white box truck. I was focused on the description of the shooters. However, I was looking for three people while others were looking for two. This whole area was in survival mode, trying to escape being killed.

On October 23rd, the FBI & ATF knocked on my door asking when was the last time I'd seen John Allen Muhammad. I told them at an emergency custody hearing in September 2001. They asked me to go to the police station for further questioning. As they were questioning me, one of the detectives said, 'Ms. Muhammad, we are going to name your ex-husband as the Sniper.' I said, 'JOHN'? I put my head down on the table. They asked, 'do you think he would do something like this?' I raised my head, looked at a corner in the room, and responded, 'yeah!' They asked why I would think that. I said, 'we were watching a movie. I don't remember the name of it, but John said he could take a small city, terrorize it. They would think it was a group of people, and it would only be him. I asked him why he would do that. He changed the subject'.

They said, 'Ms. Muhammad, didn't you know you were the target?' I said, 'no, why would I think that?' They said, 'well, he shot a man down the street from you six times, took his laptop and $3,000. He shot another man, 2 miles from you, in the abdomen. Ms. Muhammad, you were the target. They put me, my children, sister, and brother-in-law in protective custody until he was caught.

They caught him on October 25th, 2002.

He was executed on November 10th, 2009.

Conclusion

The road to healing was difficult for my children and me. I didn't find counseling for us, so I went to the library, found a book on counseling and learned to counsel myself and my children. I told them they could not use their dad as an excuse for failure.

Today, my son, John, my daughter, Salena, and my baby girl Taalibah are all doing well and are successful in their fields.

I have become a Multi-Award-Winning Global Keynote Speaker, International Expert Speaker for the US Dept. of State, Certified Consultant with the US Dept. of Justice / Office for Victims of Crime, CNN Contributor, Domestic Abuse Survivor, Certified Domestic Violence Advocate, Advisory Board Member & Public Speaking Instructor for The National Resource Center on Domestic Violence, Best-Selling Author, Trainer & Educator, Certified Professional / Personal Development Consultant and chosen to receive the 2022 WHO'S WHO IN AMERICA: ALBERT NELSON MARQUIS LIFETIME ACHIEVEMENT AWARD. I travel and speak on a global platform as the ex-wife of the DC Sniper to discuss my life of terror, abuse, and heartbreak, all while promoting Domestic Abuse/Violence Awareness and Prevention. I am recognized as "ONE OF THE NATION'S MOST POWERFUL ADVOCATES FOR VICTIMS AND SURVIVORS OF DOMESTIC VIOLENCE". WROC-TV, Rochester, NY.

www.MildredMuhammad.com

Alison Ward

Award Winning Author
and
Mental Wellness Mentor

Chapter 2

THE BEAUTIFUL GIFT IN THE UGLY BOX

By Alison Ward

As the knife glistened in the beautiful July sunshine, words were delivered that would hit me with a force, followed by blows to the head, body, and plunging knife wounds. "Today is the day you are going to die. I've planned it all.... after I've killed you, I will kill Sam". How could these words be from a man whom I once loved? The father of my son? July 5th, 1994 was the day that changed everything. A day that created pain, chaos and PTSD – Post Trauma Stress Disorder for my two-year-old son, Sam, myself, and family.

The day of The Awakening

The dawn of a new day brought hope along with the sunshine. Upon awakening, I felt warmed by the sun flooding through; there was a feeling of trepidation and anxiety that took away the feeling of lightness. I recalled that Graham wasn't going to be in our area for a few weeks. He had got a plaster restoration job in Brighton and would be staying with his brother. What a relief.

As I tended to Sam, the anxiety came back and wouldn't leave me.

It grabbed my gut and started to twist it around, coupled with a sense of nausea; no matter what I told myself, my body was telling me something totally different.

An uneventful day followed. Sam and I returned straight home from work and nursery; no park visits today. When we arrived home, we had a pleasant surprise. My sister, Emma, now just over eight months pregnant, had decided to pay us a visit. Looking tired but happy at the prospect of being a mum, Emma explained that the visit was to try and convince me to go and stay at my parents for a few days for a break. I started cooking tea whilst Emma left, and Sam watched his program.

Spag bol was on the menu tonight. If I made a large pan, I could add some extra tomatoes and it would last for two, possibly three meals. Sam loved sucking up the "worms", as we called them. He loved even more being covered in the red sauce all over his face and lips. No worries though, the bath would soon have him back to gleaming child with angelic features! A knock at the door made me jump. I must stop being so nervous, I told myself. "Scared of your own shadow," my granddad would say, how right was he now?

Imagine my surprise when opening the door to see Graham standing there.

"What are you doing here? I thought you were in Brighton?"

"I was, but I'm here now," he said. "I think we need to discuss Sam and my access".

At long last, he had realized that to be a good dad, Sam needed stability, security and routine. Maybe all my nagging had paid off. I scanned him over all too briefly and invited him in, quickly turning the gas off the spaghetti sauce as we passed the kitchen. He looked clean; his hair was washed, not greasy as it had been the last time I saw him, maybe just maybe, he's becoming more reasonable, I concluded. Imagine my surprise then, when walking into the lounge, Graham ignored Sam. How long had it been since he last saw Sam? I couldn't remember. Why is he ignoring him, I questioned silently.

As I tried to make sense of what was going on, I caught a whiff of beer. The realization hit me that "Shit", I shouldn't have let him in. I certainly wouldn't have had I smelt it upon opening the door. Remembering how violent he gets under the influence of alcohol, my anxiety returned. Feeling vulnerable and at the same time trying to work out if I needed to come up with an escape plan, I was interrupted by a sharp flash of pain. Bang! My face! Bang again! My face! No, surely this is not happening... Graham had head-butted me twice in quick succession and was now telling me, "I don't want you, but I don't want anyone else to have you."

He must have known that I was involved with someone new, a lovely man called Wayne who had literally just left for a ten-week bike trip across Europe. We connected even though we weren't looking for anyone; me out of a four-year relationship with Graham and Wayne out of a marriage. We found each other after he had made plans for this trip.

My mind started to race, is this really happening? Sam looked bewildered and frightened. My little boy, my gorgeous little boy, I couldn't stand the thought of him witnessing this. Again my thoughts were interrupted, this time by Graham's speech. "I've planned it all, I'm going to kill you. Today is the day you're going to die, and no one can help you. I know all about you and Wayne; I watched him go. Today is the day that you are going to die and you will be all alone, no one will find you. Then I'm going to kill me and Sam." "No, please", I shrieked, "God no, not Sam. I'll do anything, please Graham, please, please!"

By now, blood was pouring from my lips; the top one had split in two. Graham proceeded to tell me about his plan, he informed me that no one knew he was here, and he had alibis who would state that he was with them, his brother in Brighton being one of them. The torture had well and truly begun! I had to think and quickly; out of the corner of my eye, I could see Sam starting to react; a panic set in. Then a glint of a knife interrupted my thoughts.

Graham had produced a knife from his back pocket. "He means this; he really means this," I told myself. My dream was true, Gail's cards and recent tarot reading were true, and my gut instincts were true. Today is really the day I'm going to die. Twenty-nine years old!

So many thoughts, so many fears tumbled down all at once. As I was trying to work out what to do, another head butt came down. This time in full force, he then repeatedly banged my head against the wall. By now, Graham had manoeuvred me into the corner and was straddled across me; trapped, with no escape. My head started to swim, and consciousness slipped away; I could see the knife; it was now in front of my face. This was the knife that had been missing from my kitchen drawer; how long had he planned this?

The next stage was inevitable; he started to stab at my chest. The piercing pain gripped me as the blood shot across the room in short sharp bursts. So many things happening all at once; was I watching a horror movie? I wasn't sure. The reality hit me; it was a horror movie, and we were the main cast. I knew I had to somehow remain conscious. If I gave into the fear and pain, we would surely die; it would be too easy to kill me and Sam, my baby, my God, my baby! I'm his mum, it's my job to protect him.

Naturally yet quite bizarrely, I started to sing nursery rhymes in my head, "Hickory, Dickory dock, the mouse ran up the clock..." trying to focus on each word; then yet another blow reminded me I was being killed, murdered in front of my little boy, two and a half years old. Sam decided he had to help; he jumped on Graham's back, telling him to stop, "Daddy no!" My brave boy kicked and punched his Dad with all his might.

Begging Sam to move away so he wouldn't fall victim to the knife with a job to do, he did as I told him to do! Sam continued to try so many other things, all to no avail. He placed my glasses next to me that I used to watch TV, but that didn't work, so he fetched his precious dressing gown belt that he used to suck and place in the corner of his eye when he felt sleepy. Graham paid no attention to him; he just kept on going. Sam then let out a howling animal-like noise, then fled to his potty where he sat, again trying to deflect Graham's attention.

I could see all this even in the midst of this horrific ordeal. By this time, I had brought my leg up to protect my heart and chest and felt the knife penetrate deep into my shin area, I knew my time was coming to an end, I felt myself succumb to the blood seeping and shooting from my body, and I became very woozy.

This wooziness leads to me somehow leaving my body…

My near-death experience brought me back home with a renewed sense of self and purpose. Sam and I were diagnosed with PTSD, Graham was charged with two counts of attempted murder. Thirteen months later, his charges were lessened, and he served eighteen months of a three-year sentence in an open prison where he got 'fit'- that was a message from his probation officer who chose to call me "Al" and presumed I welcomed this disrespectful approach.

The aftermath was desperate; we lost our home, my job, and our peace of mind. The one thing that once it has gone, you crave for its return. I felt invisible. Unheard. Judged. Unseen. Dismissed.

We were all over the news and local newspaper, radio, and rumours spread like a forest fire. "I can see why he did it to you, but why Sam?" was one remark by a so-called friend. Remarks like that from another female were just the start of the shocking aftermath from 'friends' and society. People assumed that I deserved this treatment in some bizarre way.

—

We had to go into hiding as Graham got bail and used this position to return to our hometown, even though he wasn't allowed as part of his bail conditions.

Everything I had believed in was smashed to pieces, I became paranoid and didn't know whom to trust, even suspecting my nearest and dearest.

Thank God this was short-lived, just part of the PTSD journey.

Wayne returned home from his bike trip on the eve of my 30th birthday In September. Even though I had no expectations (Sam was my number one priority), we reconnected, bonded, and somehow have stayed together ever since.

The new, improved version of me was a strong, feisty woman with amazing intuition and spiritual connection, a newfound wisdom, and a gift to be able to read energy, people's thoughts and be solutions focused in a practical way. I have spent the last twenty-four years creating a methodology and business that got me well, happy and calm. It's called Bringing You Back To YOU and is the name of my second book.

The tools I share were given to me after The Awakening via thoughts, dreams, meditations and clear guidance. I have passed them on to thousands of people through my books, courses, one-to-one sessions and media appearances. It has brought me a deep sense of worth and fulfilment and has saved and enhanced lives.

Sam is thriving. He is a successful thirty-year-old events creative director with a large sports brand and is kicking ass in his own individual way. Wayne and I have celebrated twenty-six years of marriage and have enjoyed being pregnant and bringing our son, James into the world, a thriving athlete, marathon runner, YouTube creator and engineer.

It hasn't been easy to create a happy life, a life of peace and calm in the midst of chaos. We have been affected in so many ways, financially being one that was unexpected, mentally, and emotionally yet developed us all spiritually. We have worked together as a family of values – truth. Integrity, open communication, love and humour. Whenever an awkward question has been asked, wherever we may have been, we have answered it honestly.

We never called Graham horrible names; the power of pause and silence is a great tool. We decided that the boys would create their own views, and they have. We have always encouraged the boys to be open and honest with how they are feeling, to be emotionally intelligent, to be expressive, creative, and 'Dare To Dreamers'. Encouraged them to not follow the crowd and be their own unique, brilliant person.

You can imagine the air in our home has sometimes been full of angry words released so they don't fester, laughter and oh so bad jokes, yet also hugs, lots of hugs. An open house to their friends who have become our friends now they are adults.

Our story is known as 'Domestic Abuse', yet we had left Graham and started a new life. He decided that even though he didn't want me, no one else could have me. Sadly, a cliché that is a proven statistic. Not all Domestic Abuse situations happen when the relationship is still a union; many happen after the other has left the home. Abuse takes many forms; being emotionally distant is a form of abuse, holding back and controlling money another. Name-calling, insinuations, gaslighting as well as the obvious hitting and hurting.

I experienced all the above, no doubt scarred for life, but I decided, enough was enough. I deserve to live and be happy. Every day I do 'the inner work', make a difference in my unique way and strive to be a grateful and better version each day. I start and end the day with five new gratitudes. I allow myself to process emotional pin when it arises.

I am surrounded by people who 'get' me, love and support me. I am OK with saying "no!" I make mistakes, but don't beat myself up when I do, instead choosing to see 'lessons learned'.

My advice to you, dear reader is; listen to the whispers, your gut feeling, the red flags alerting you. If you are shown a red flag early on in a relationship, please do not ignore it in this heady, yummy phase of a new relationship. It is there to warn you so stop! Listen, observe and be truly honest if you don't like what you see. Take the appropriate action. This will end your cycle of abuse.

Learn to trust and value you, your life and values. You are worthy, loved and valuable. The world needs awakened, empathetic souls. Get to know you, your values and only align to others who mirror your values. Don't be afraid to disappoint another if they do not value you. And most importantly, the best form of revenge is happiness. This is the story of the beautiful gift in the ugly box.

Love you
Alison Ward

www.alison-ward.co.uk
linktree://linktr.ee/AlisonWardMentor

Ana Williams

Speaker
Author
Founder of AMA Legacy LLC

Chapter 3

ENCHANTED WITH MY ENEMY

By Ana Williams

I was subjected to mental, physical, and verbal abuse.

All of this began when we chose to marry and moved together across the street from my oldest sister's house in Los Angeles, California, in the summer of 1992. I moved in with him and was overjoyed because I thought I had found my Prince Charming and that this was true love. I made up a story about how wonderful and perfect my life and marriage would be because he was very kind and lovely, and he would reach the stars and bring one to me. On the other hand, he was spontaneous and told me within an hour or two that we would be flying out of the state. I used to be so excited and joyful about traveling that it didn't matter whether I was flying or driving. I grew up in a highly impoverished family and never had anything. So, this was new to me because I used to think he was an incredible man who would shower me with all kinds of gifts at once, like clothes, shoes, flowers, money, you name it.

He was lovely and always there for my family and friends. I was willing to trust anything he said. When I first met his family, one thing that struck me was what his mother told him: "Be good to Ana; she is the nicest thing that could ever happen in your life," I smiled, I felt flattered because she genuinely liked me. When she informed him, I was overjoyed, but I couldn't understand why she had to say that to him. We were heading back to his house, and he was delighted that his mother had embraced my son and me.

So, life went on, and he continued to surprise me with his friends' throwing parties at his house, and he would take me to all kinds of engagements. I was amazed when he would introduce me to his friends and show me off. I was too preoccupied with his charm to notice any signs of abuse. He was always smiling from ear to ear and cracking jokes. He was very brilliant to me! For all I knew, he didn't want me to notice the subtle signs of abuse, so he was showering me with all kinds of wonderful gifts. I was unaware that I was in the hands of a beast.

Where is My Prince Charming?
Everything was fine until we moved from across the street from my sister to another location in Los Angeles; after that, I could not visit my mother as frequently. If I went to see her, the house phone would ring minutes after I arrived. My mom would ask, "Is there any reason your man is calling you so much?" He loves

me, misses being with me, and likes being with me. I responded that there were no particular reasons.

According to my mother, "that makes no sense because you just left your house, he can't possibly miss you that much when you only live 20 minutes away". I began to believe what my mother had told me was true.

It became worse over time. I noticed that he would call my job, and the phone would ring the moment I stepped inside. It was sweet at first to have someone constantly checking on me.

However, my boss warned me to be cautious with him since he wasn't sure if he was a good fit for me and was concerned about my relationship with him. I didn't listen to anyone, I feared many people would dislike him because he was black. I didn't listen to my friends or anyone else at the time.

However, something wasn't quite right. Something inside me was telling me to pay attention, and I was becoming concerned because I knew deep down in my heart that this man was controlling me more with each passing day. So, one day, I decided to ask him a question, I was afraid that he would become enraged, but I mustered the guts to do so. I asked, "Why do you call me so much? I don't like it. It is weird that you are calling to check on me. I feel like you don't trust me. It is so embarrassing; my friends and family think it is not normal for you to call everywhere I go. They think you are freaking controlling me. Stop making me appear awful, and stop calling me names. You are behaving like you have crazy control over me. I don't like it, and I'm not lying to you, so please stop it. It's because I'm meant to be at the location where I said I'd be." I asked, "Could you perhaps clarify this to me? It worries me that all my friends and family have seen the same pattern!"

He became enraged and urged me to shut up, explaining that he checked on me because he loved me and only checked to ensure I was safe.

After a few weeks, he began to dictate who I spoke to on the phone, who I visited, and who could visit me. So as time passed, he gained more control over me, to the point where I had to stop visiting my friends because he was jealous and upset about everything. I remember being unable to speak because I was afraid of making him angry. I also quit my job because he did not want me to work anymore, and then I became pregnant.

It was a nightmare. I already had a three-year-old kid who was not his. Initially he was nice to my son, but then he became mean to him as well. I was trapped because I was pregnant and ashamed that I was with an abuser. I didn't want anyone to know that he was consistently abusing me. I was also suffering for my son, and it was painful to know that my little boy had to see his mother being hit.

My son was also beaten, and I used to feel hopeless. I felt like it was my fault. I used to think that I deserved this abuse because I did it to myself. I didn't tell anyone I was being abused, no friends, no family, because he made sure that I was isolated from anyone who could help me. He planned to keep me away from all my friends and family.

I felt helpless, blaming myself every day and night, and he would talk down to me. When I was pregnant with my first daughter, I couldn't tell him it was a girl because he would be angry since he wanted a boy. So, I was trapped with no hope and no one to talk to; I felt ashamed of myself because it was my fault for not noticing the signs. I was heartbroken and refused to accept anything. I would pray to God for help. I was pregnant and alone with a son while he was out, enjoying sleeping with as many women as possible. He was a popular guy, so many females adored him. I'd get calls from women telling me they were sleeping with him.

My life had been shattered. I had a child on the way and a son who needed me, so I had to pray and ask God to give me the strength I needed to get through each day until he released me from the hands of a beast.

He went to the ultrasound when he found out I was pregnant with a girl rather than a boy. I already knew it was a girl, but I hid it from him because I knew he would be furious. Sure enough, he yelled at me, calling me names, and I cried in the car, not saying anything since it was only going to get worse. I remember that it was early in the day, and as I write this chapter on 02/14/2022 at 3:38 pm, it still hurts so terribly.

When we got home, he dropped me off and returned to work. I got down on my knees and prayed again, asking God to calm him down so he wouldn't be too unhappy when he returned home after work. He knew I was hiding the fact that I was carrying a lovely princess inside of me. I adored my daughter from the day I conceived her, just as I adored my firstborn.

He returned home and remained silent, so I stayed quiet. After abusing me, he was the type of man who would return with a gift so that I could forgive him, and he always vowed that he would not hurt me again. I learnt the pattern, and at first, I believed it, but it was a deception; he would continue to torture me. I used to give the gifts away to my neighbors since they reminded me of my pain.

One day, my next-door neighbor saw him beating me, grabbed a broom, and smacked him, telling him to stop and that he should be ashamed of assaulting a woman: oh my! I was relieved that someone had noticed but terrified because I knew what would happen behind closed doors. I had no idea how to get back into the house because this man was 6 feet 5 inches tall. So, I waited outside the home until I figured out how to deal with what was about to happen. When I got inside, he was waiting for me in the dark bedroom, my heart was about to explode with fear of him hurting me again.

Existence was so difficult, if you can call it that, I was in constant agony, not knowing if I would live or die and that any day may be the end of my life.

Learning to deal with an abusive partner was difficult initially, but ultimately you adapt to the abuse and learn to cope with suffering. I learned how to handle my situation so I would not go insane or kill myself.

When you understand who this monster is and what he was capable of doing to me, both physically and mentally. Let me tell you, I was humiliated and mistreated for years. I was fat. I didn't care how I looked. I didn't care about anything but my kids. I would eat at night when he went to bed. It was a challenge. I had to pretend to be happy no matter what was happening; I had to learn how to survive, knowing I had children to love and protect.

Getting up every day next to a man who makes you wonder whether this is the last day of your life. I used to wonder, will he injure me if I fall asleep? My life was uncertain the entire time I lived with him.

I began to pray more and more, learning that my only refuge was God. I would read the bible to learn of his promises, knowing that one day he would rescue me from the hands of this evil man. Smiling was difficult, but I learned to keep a fake smile inside. The only joy I remember was seeing my children safe, not knowing if they would be okay if this man would take my life.

I'd pray and ask God to protect me and grant me life. I didn't want it for myself. I only wanted to ensure that my children had a safe place to live. I wanted to flee, but my mind wasn't ready. He enslaved me, and there was no way I could ever escape. For so many years, he told me I was nothing without him, that no one cared or would ever love me as much as him.

I didn't understand anything; I knew I was used to being abused and that there was no way out for me.

Purple Eye

I was severely emotionally affected; I was not happy and constantly anxious; my life was robbed; I transformed into a different person; I was severely sad and suffered from anxiety attacks. I'd put on a lot of weight. My identity had been stolen, and I had no idea what it felt like to be me again. It was strange because I was a pleasant, outgoing person. When I was able to go to church, I had to wear sunglasses and put a lot of make-up on to hide my purple eye.

When I went to church, I would cry and beg God to help me escape this chaotic life. I wanted to be in a secure place with my kids, and I needed help, but I didn't know who to ask because it was taboo, and I couldn't tell anyone anything. I was embarrassed and ashamed about my life and telling anyone was not on my agenda. It was very sad how he manipulated me. I was under him with no money of my own, no work, and no way to help myself. I had no friends to talk to. I had a family, but I didn't want them to know because it was too painful. They lived in Los Angeles, and I moved to Florida with him in 1998. I was too far away for them to help me. On the other hand, Mom was a wise mother, and she had my brother phone the cops to check on me as she was anxious because I hadn't been able to speak with her in a long time.

When the cops knocked on the door, my ex-husband opened it. I became concerned because I had no idea what was happening. Then, when I arrived at the door, they asked if I was okay, and I said I was and I added, "May I ask why are you here? I never contacted the cops."

They told me my mother had phoned them because she was worried about me and wanted to know why I hadn't called her. They asked if I was okay, and I told them I was. I also told them that my phone was broken but that I would contact her as soon as I fixed it; they responded okay.

The officers went away, and my ex-husband became enraged. He began doing what he does best: hitting me. I remembered him putting a pillow in my face for a long time until I couldn't breathe, then letting go until I was weak and able to breathe again. I had blood spots on my skin and my face, which made me look like I had chickenpox; it was terrible, but I thank God I could breathe again.

The Strategy

There's a lot more to say about my experience, but I can tell you that I carefully plotted my escape. I continued to take the abuse. I kept in mind that I needed to devise an escape strategy. Well, two weeks before my escape, his stepmother called me and asked if I was okay. I told her no, I wasn't okay, and I explained the situation to her. She said she would help me if I ever decided to leave, and I thanked her. I believe God had answered my prayers at that moment, I was crying with joy because I knew my escape was near.

The same week she called me, I felt like an angel came to visit me while I was sleeping; it was late at night when I felt someone touch my shoulder and heard a voice saying everything was going to be okay. I jumped out of bed. I was terrified, thinking this man was going to kill me tonight. I ran to his room, but he was sleeping. I calmed myself. It was time to act and escape.

That time came when the opportunity of a lifetime presented itself, but I was terrified. I became so weak that I couldn't breathe, just thinking about how he could harm all of us if he found out I was planning to flee with the kids. That night, he was very upset with me, and all I remembered was that he had a machete and was hitting the floor, telling me that he was going to hurt me. So that night, I called the police from my house, then I hung up, hoping that the police would not call back but would show up at my home without me having to speak to them.

They came and told me I had to leave or I would die here tonight, so I did. It was difficult because I had no idea where I was going, no money, no job, no skill, no self-esteem, and no identity. I stopped for a minute and said, "no, I can't leave because I don't have anything." But my oldest son told me you believe in God, so don't be afraid. Let's go, mom; God will help us. That's all I needed, a push, and we left.

Just remember that you must believe in yourself, that you must ask for help, that you must talk to a friend or family member, and that you must not make the same mistakes I did. It's time to speak up! You need to know that there are a lot of resources available.

All you need is a strategy and the confidence to act. We are here to be loved, not to be exploited or harmed. Now that I've moved on, I've become a professional speaker against domestic violence. I've also worked as a Director and Associate Director of Financial Aid for HCI College for the past few years.

Last year, PELOTON invited me to perform a global video in Spanish to train their employees by sharing a portion of MY narrative about domestic violence to help women like me so that we can help others. I've also given talks in local churches and other venues. I'm overjoyed to know that I'm assisting others.

Dionne Joi

Holistic Wellness and Mindset
Transformation Coach
Founder of Joi Luck Club

Chapter 4

JOI AND PAIN

By Dionne Joi

IN THE BEGINNING...

If you had asked me when I was younger if I thought I would be somebody special, I would've said no. I didn't grow up with a silver spoon and didn't even think I would get my happy ending.

For most of my life, I have dealt with severe depression. I have experienced anxiety and suicidal thoughts. There were times when I felt so alone, sad, and detached that I didn't think I wanted to keep going. Now I feel like I have experienced the worst and can recover from whatever life throws my way.

At a young age, I suffered abuse. I was touched a few times. When I was in middle school, I was raped by a boy from school. I was afraid to tell anyone. When I was 16, I was so unhappy I drank so much alcohol that I almost died from alcohol poisoning. I didn't realize I was depressed. My mom thought I was a typical teenager, but I was hurting.

Go figure!

Then at 17, I got pregnant. My water broke when I was 19 weeks. I had to live in a hospital for five weeks, on bed rest, to save my baby. I went into labor at 24 weeks and gave birth to my baby boy who died about 2 hours later. His name was Carlos. He would have been 21 on May 14th. That trauma caused more depression, and my fragile teenage brain could not comprehend such a loss.

It felt like I'd always had to be in survivor mode and prepare for something to go wrong. Everyone had let me down, it seems. I'm not even sharing everything that has happened to me, but I know my entire story will make for a great movie one day.

Many things that happened to me resemble scenes from a tragic movie. No wonder I was so depressed. There was so much I had to deal with while pretending everything was fine.

No one knew what I had to deal with or what I was going through. I suppressed so much pain and anger and didn't know how to cope. My innocence was stolen from me. I was lost with no direction and so many questions.

What was love? What does a real relationship look like? Why is life this way? Will I ever be happy? I would figure it out.

WHAT HAD HAPPENED

It wasn't until recently that I started to reflect on my life to understand who I am and why I experienced certain things. It's hard to believe that I was once unhappy. It's also harder to believe that I now know that I deserve to be happy!

For as long as I can remember, I have lived with the fact that this is just how my life will be. I settled for mediocrity. I didn't believe in myself. I was looking for love from the outside because I didn't love myself, so I settled for any man that gave me attention. I attracted narcissists and people who used me. I hung around people who didn't add value to my life to feel a connection. I didn't put my needs first. I was a mess. I know that now. I was told I was too hard and was called crazy. Some said I was too nice. I craved attention and acceptance because my self-esteem was so low. I thought men only wanted one thing and that relationships were bullshit. But those feelings and thoughts stemmed from something much deeper. I was living in a distorted reality and had lived in pain for so long.

I used to think that arguing with your loved one was normal. Looking back, that should have been my first sign. But at 19, I didn't understand that, and I just wanted to be loved.

Now I realize that people who argue and yell lack self-control and don't know how to express their thoughts and emotions.

57

So, in my seemingly good relationship with my ex, there was a lot of arguing and yelling when we didn't see eye to eye. The first physical contact was outside of his house at the time. We argued. He pushed my forehead with his pointer and middle finger. We had broken up a few times during our entire relationship.

One night my ex and I were on a date, and on the way back, another friend called me. That didn't go very well. He got on the phone with the other guy at some point, and they had words. My ex got so mad. We started arguing in the car as he was driving me home. As we got off the exit, he scraped the side of the wall driving recklessly. I was so scared. I yelled at him to pull over so I could get out of the car. I remembered thinking that he would crash the car. He pulled over to let me out. I didn't realize that my friend was still on the phone and had heard the whole thing. He stayed on the phone while I walked to a nearby late-night spot that was open and had people outside. One of the people saw me get out of the car and called me a cab to get home.

The next time I remember vividly. My ex was staying at my place while I was at work. I remember coming home and not feeling well. I was feeling sick and tired the whole day, so when I got home, the first thing I did was lay on the couch. He was in the bedroom. He heard me come in. I remember him telling me to "COME HERE." I told him I wasn't feeling well and had to lie down. He told me again he wanted me to go back to the room. I honestly didn't have the energy to get up, so I told him to get up and come to the living room. That incited an argument that I wasn't prepared for. It was so bad; I told him to leave. He insisted that he would not leave, so I called the police. He was yelling. He said he would leave and went to grab his TV. As I was following him out, he punched me in the face, grabbed the TV and left.

The phone dropped to the floor while still talking to the police, I picked it up and they said they had heard the whole thing and were on their way. As I spoke to the officer in my home, he notified me that they had located my ex and told me to see a doctor. The next day, I went to the doctor's office to examine my injuries. After my check-up, they told me I was pregnant, which explains why I wasn't feeling well.

Shortly after, I told my ex we were having a baby. Even though my ex was not there for the birth of our daughter, we ended up back together again. I wanted to work it out so I could have a family because that's what we wanted. We were young, and neither knew what a real relationship was. But the last straw was the incident when our daughter was not even two years old.

We were living together at this time. Things weren't going well. We were both unhappy. One night I was fed up with him not being home, and as it got later and later, I became even more upset. After about 10 pm, I put the chain on the door so he couldn't get in. He had been ignoring my calls, texts, and voicemails.

My final message to him was not to come back tonight. I called his mom, looking for him. I told her to let him know that he shouldn't come back that night. I was awakened in the middle of the night by a banging on the door. Guess who was home? I had to let him in. I told him I didn't want him sleeping in the bed with me because I felt disrespected.

Of course, he didn't listen; he went to bed and lay beside me. I kept telling him to get out and to leave me alone. He didn't, and he said something disrespectful. I started pushing him out of bed with my hands and feet telling him to leave. I was fed up at this point. He grabbed my feet and dragged me to the end of the bed, grabbed me, and turned me on my stomach. He got on top of me and held my head to the pillow. He then pulled my arm behind my back and told me that he would break my arm. At this point, I was waiting for him to do it.

Our one-and-a-half-year-old daughter came into the room and screamed, **"STOP, DADDY!"** To this day, I'm still not sure how much she saw. Luckily, my son from a previous relationship wasn't home that night to witness any of this.

Our daughter crying and yelling caused him to stop and get up. He grabbed her and picked her up. I grabbed my phone, ran to the bathroom, locked myself inside, and called the police to remove him from our place. I called his mother and my mother to come over. He left with his mom that night. I had to get a restraining order so he couldn't return to our place. After that, I vowed never again to put myself or my children in another position.

We never got back together.

I didn't want our arguments to continue to escalate. I knew I didn't want my children to grow up in a toxic environment. I had already been through so much that I wasn't in a good mental space. There I was, at 22, a single mom of two, and now you can add survivor of domestic violence to the list.

THE HEALING PROCESS IS SO THERAPEUTIC

I didn't seek help for many of my past issues when I was younger. I was going through life in pain and mental anguish most of the time. My value was diminished, or so I thought. My standards were low. Besides my two children, I didn't have anything to live for. I had suppressed so much of what had happened to me that I didn't realize it affected how I lived my life. I buried so many of my stories so deep so as to forget them instead of dealing with them. After all, I was a child. I didn't have anyone to talk to about what had happened. I didn't trust people and thought I couldn't be loved.

I was hurting on the inside, and because that feeling was "normal", I didn't realize I needed help. I had toxic thoughts and behavior like others who have dealt with trauma. I attracted other toxic people into my life as well. Even when people surrounded me, I felt lonely.

No one knew me. I was ashamed, embarrassed, hurt, and angry. For so long, sadness was a part of my life. I know I'm not the only person who feels that way.

It wasn't until I started healing that I changed my view of myself. As I changed for the better, so did my environment. The healing process is so therapeutic. Releasing energy that no longer serves you brings you inner peace. Once I decided I wanted and deserved to be happy, the universe started cooperating with me.

I now have better relationships and attract only those who align with my energy. I let go of all toxic people and surround myself with positive people. I now attract and receive love because I love myself, and that's the energy I put out. I now allow myself to be happy and am not defined by my past.

My ex and I co-parent our daughter and have no issues now. I have forgiven him. After all, it was years ago, and we have since moved on and grown up. I don't live in fear. I am so glad that part of my life is over.

IT'S TIME TO HEAL

Like a rose that grew from the concrete, I, too, could still blossom despite everything I had to overcome. And man, oh man, how my mindset and life have changed. Who would have thought I could walk around with a smile, be happy, and make a living helping people love life again?

I made a commitment to myself never to let anyone else steal my joy! I am in control of my life, and I feel so empowered. I am now a certified reiki master, aromatherapist, holistic wellness coach, motivational speaker, and author. I use my experience and knowledge to teach and help other people change their mindsets so that they can change their lives. I launched my company **JOI LUCK CLUB,** and my passion lies in speaking love, spreading joy, and sharing knowledge.

I used to think so little of myself. Now I have people tell me how inspiring I am. I help other people heal, and I love it. I am living

---

proof that things can get better. I have had some amazing experiences, and more opportunities are always coming up. Life is what we make it. I've spent too much time being unhappy. I refuse to do that again.

My children need me to be the best version of myself. I am so happy that I can be present for them while being happy! They have witnessed my transformation into the woman I am now. It means the world when they tell me they're proud of me. Of course, with teenagers, you don't always see eye to eye, but I cherish every moment. I can teach them strength, determination, and a positive mindset, and I am doing all I can for them. I never gave up on myself or them. I am proud of myself and all of my accomplishments.

One thing we all have in common is pain. Pain is inevitable, but misery is a choice. I choose joy. Everyone experiences pain at some point in life. The key to being happy is choosing not to stay in that pain. To embrace it, learn from it, and use it to improve.

It hurts to go through horrible things, but making it through and not letting your past get the best of you is the most empowering feeling you will ever have. Remember, you've already gone through it; now it's time to heal from it.

Jacqueline Miller

Speaker
Author
Training Facilitator

Chapter 5

CURATING HEALTH ADVERSITIES

By Jacqueline Miller

For the past 20-plus years, I curated my adverse childhood and health experiences by turning them into opportunities to address domestic and sexual violence and systemic change.

One day, I talked with my mother while taking down my braids. She told me my hair had grown fast when I was a girl. At that moment, I remembered that my hair was extremely thin and bald on the sides at different points in my life. I planned to work on the bald spots with all I learned about managing stress and self-care. I learned about essential oils and tested different ones on my skin. I had positive results and decided to try them on the bald areas of my head. My mom celebrated with me when I showed her that hair was growing in those areas.

I was motivated to tune into my inner voice. My confidence in beginning my healing journey deepened. I remembered that one of the domestic violence programs I worked for had a self-help philosophical approach. I was inspired to create my healing journey, which consisted of self-help tools.

I permitted myself to change my customized self-healing plan at any moment and any time. I looked deep within myself to define what self-care meant to me. It was more than getting massages and going to spas. I took a path of self-discovery, which consisted of rites of passage programs and practices of various healing modalities rooted in my ancestral culture.

As I began writing this chapter, I noted that the chaos I experienced during my childhood had not seeped into my spirit. Although I was uncertain about the future, I remained hopeful about it. I have crossed the paths of many people who felt that children who have gone through domestic and sexual violence were damaged forever. Let me tell you how untrue this is.

There was no organization, no pastor, no officer, no teacher and no doctor who put me on this healing journey. Very few recognized that I was experiencing domestic and sexual abuse, mostly because I was quiet, an A student, talented, a happy child and always clean and well dressed. I needed the time, space and determined spirit to launch my healing at full speed. It was my time to fully curate my health adversities and explore opportunities to bring about systemic change on behalf of survivors and their children.

After learning about intergenerational trauma, I asked my mother to tell me her story.

While she shared, I also learned about my grandmother's traumatic experiences. Now, trauma has shown up in my life.

For years, I hid my experiences of sexual abuse because I knew things would get worse if I told my mother about it.

My suffering with asthma for many years did not make it easier to tell my mother about the sexual abuse. She and I spent every other weekend together riding the public bus to the hospital. My asthma was so severe that I wondered if I would ever get to play ball, jump rope, ride a bicycle and skateboard as other children did. Imagine a child who contends with life-threatening illnesses every day due to environmental harms, allergies to carpet, pests and cigarette smoke, not to mention the stress from witnessing domestic violence regularly.

Without drawing from my childhood experiences of domestic and sexual abuse, I followed my heart and pursued volunteering at a domestic violence shelter. I knew my purpose was more significant and rooted in serving those abused and mistreated. The time came when my compassion, empathy, love for humanity and previous work experiences all came together and led me to the path of the gender-based violence movement. Thirty-plus years in the movement, I am here and thriving.

I curated the chaos from the innumerable chaotic years and demonstrated my leadership abilities. I reframed the adversities and disorder by building resilience. More leadership opportunities came forth.

During many summer breaks from school when I was young, I gathered neighborhood children on our front porch and conducted my first summer camp. I taught lessons on unity, resolving conflict, and how to take care of our neighborhood. I enjoyed being outside and spending time with nature.

Within the gender-based violence movement, I learned you are either part of the solution or part of the problem. Wanting to be part of the solution, I drew from my childhood organizing skills and ran a six-week summer camp for children. This was my second one to run with my finances. I wanted to create more safe spaces for children.

As a Black woman doing advocacy work for more than half of my life, this movement has benefitted from my being here. My commitment to serving survivors has widened over the years, and I continue to identify areas where we can improve our response to the violence that children are exposed to. One of the areas that I cultivated within the movement nationally is addressing the adultification of children with an emphasis on Black girls.

Adultification is when children take on adult roles or are held to the same standards as adults. I was adultified in many ways. I took on the role of protecting my mother and my siblings. There were also many ways I was adultified by society which was of no support for what I was experiencing at home.

As I have developed addressing adultification within the gender-based violence movement, I reflected on my many childhood experiences.

The emergency room seemed to be one of the few places where adults would welcome me with open arms and smiles up until I turned a teenager. Before then, they addressed me as a child. The doctors were careful with me and would get on my level to look me in the eye. Shortly after turning 13, they stopped looking me in the eyes and rarely said hello.

They would listen to my chest to find the wheezing, and with no eye contact, they would leave the room and send a nurse in with medication.

I felt two things when my mother and I walked through the hospital doors. I felt relieved that the wheezing would stop and that my air passages would be cleared. At the time, I was using an over-the-counter inhaler to bring immediate relief and the opening of my lungs.

There were many times that I was out of my inhaler. This was when I learned that adults with power and resources could easily manipulate children and take complete advantage of them. A family friend, who knew I was out of my inhaler, offered to bring me one if I performed oral sex on her. I was so scared. Being 12 years old, I had no clue what she meant. Many studies show that Black girls are perceived to be more knowledgeable about sex and adult topics than girls of any other race. The truth is I was viewed the same way as Black girls are today.

The weekend after this offer, my mother had to take me to E.R. for another severe asthma attack. I was admitted to the hospital. During my stay, the security guard who flirted with me while I was in E.R. came to my room, closed my door and sexually assaulted me. No one intervened.

Although there wasn't much to my bedroom, I could not wait to get home and return to bed. There wasn't much in my bedroom. Besides being shared by my younger sister, it had a closet full of clothes made by my mother. Besides the closet, I remember it had a 6-foot narrow window. The window faced a brick wall to the south of us. The view was pale and lifeless. No sun ever shone there. This is another time that I reflected on my unbroken spirit and remained hopeful. I knew that the brick wall wasn't the end.

My love for art contributed to my hope for a brighter future. My natural talent for art received an honorable mention by one of my high school art teachers. This was the moment that I learned that abusers often emotionally abuse children by destroying what they create. The same often happens to adult survivors. A lot of my projects, such as an embroidered pillow, paintings and paper dolls, were destroyed by my mother's abuser. He commented that it was only junk and good for the trash. Sometimes, he also put my homework assignments in the garbage. I soon learned not to work at the kitchen table and to only do my homework in my bedroom, which did not have sufficient light.

Speaking of the kitchen table, I was often denied food and not allowed to sit with my siblings as they were allowed to eat. He would share the rice he cooked with them but told me that I had to wait for my mother to get home from work. I trained myself to hate rice and not to be hungry after school.

This healing work that I've done has resulted in me now loving rice. Yes, rice! Sometimes, I even crave it. I have thought about joining hunger movements, but once again, I am thinking of more ways to connect the dots of hunger to the gender-based violence movement.

I discovered my level of resilience and how I never settled for not having a solution to a problem. I continued to search for ways to heal on my own since there seemed not to have been safe places or adults to turn to. I started writing and found ways to hide my works so they wouldn't be destroyed. I never wrote about the abuse that I was experiencing. I wrote poems and short stories about mysteries, love and the future. Later, I started writings stage plays. One of my plays became a script and a curriculum for my second summer camp for children. I remember one of the parents of a summer camp participant shared that his son struggled with reading. At the end of the camp performance, the parent shared how excited his son was when he brought the script home. He told his dad that he's "reading scripts now." I modeled how loving adults can create opportunities to be part of the solution, not the problem.

At various times, I give thought to how my life may have turned out if I had been removed from my mother. This thought is devasting. There is a belief that children's lives would be improved if they were removed from homes where domestic violence occurs. Based on my experience, I beg to differ. Although unfortunate, I attribute much of my growth to those adverse childhood experiences.

Throughout this work, I have learned that not all intervention is healthy or the best approach. Some interventions have silenced survivors, mandated them for services and even made them responsible for the harm. It is critical to include the voices of survivors in all interventions rather than not respecting their autonomy.

With this in mind, I created Healthy Actions Intervening Responsibly (H.A.I.R.). Through H.A.I.R., I launched raising awareness of the many areas of children's lives that impact their overall well-being and health. Domestic violence is one; adultification is another, and now I will expound on one other.

I drew from my lived experiences of threatening to be killed regularly. For six years, I led a reducing intimate homicide project which mobilized a coordinated community response approach designed to increase safety nets for survivors and their children. Through this work, I developed leadership skills around leading harm reduction work while centering on survivors, their children and their safety. I identified areas where systemic responses and approaches could be improved. I discovered many ways that the child welfare system and batterers intervention programs could reframe their practices in a less criminalized and punitive manner.

This became one of my most appreciated experiences within the movement. I found that not many people were aware of the lethality risk factors for survivors who had a child that was not the biological child of their abuser.

I recognize that there is room for more opportunities within our movement to create buffers and protective factors that can help to eliminate a child's self-esteem being torn down as it relates to their art, bodies, sense of worth, and what the future can hold for them.

Every day I learn more and more about the impact and outcomes of trauma resulting from domestic and sexual abuse. This is an ongoing learning journey, even when living in a home free of violence.

A lot of healing has taken place within my memory. My creative capacity has been expanded. I recently took out the eighth-grade graduation photo that I had buried. It held so many painful memories. I looked her in the eyes and affirmed her. I told her how brave and strong she was. I introduced her to her adult self and told her that she survived one hundred percent of those chaotic days. Now, my future holds a world of opportunities for telling my story of resilience through photography.

As a lead racial equity and social change worker at a national organization, I am eager for the world to hear from another adult who survived childhood exposure to domestic and sexual violence. Violence and tactics of abuse are man-made. No one is born an abuser. We know this because it is a learned behavior.

Just as violence is man-made, hunger is man-made, and so is racism. These are all rooted in oppression. Unfortunately, many of us experience these forms of oppression based on the color of our skin.

I am glad to know that my spirit endured the chaotic moments and tides of childhood adverse experiences of domestic violence and sexual abuse. My spirit has not been broken by adversity. It has been reawakened and renewed by what I knew all along, "you will not just survive, but you will thrive" through it all.

I attribute one hundred percent of my healing to leaning in on my hope and faith, my culture, the rites of passage program that I sought out and Black affinity spaces within the movement that acknowledges and welcomes the brilliance of Black women who lead with their survivorship and beyond.

I will continue to create opportunities for my younger self to take the next decade, sharing her story of Curating Health Adversities for Opportunities of Systemic Change so that someone else's chaos can be transformed and reframed.

Johan Rylander

Author
Spokesperson for men who are
exposed to domestic violence
Public Speaker

Chapter 6

DOMESTIC VIOLENCE HAS NO GENDER

By Johan Rylander

Introduction

June 27th, 2018. My 13-year-old son and I are arriving by train in Stockholm. We are experiencing the hottest summer in ages. All around us, we see happy and excited people. People are wearing Swedish national soccer t-shirts. Waiving Swedish flags. World Cup in soccer is on, and Sweden is playing against Mexico this evening.

Everything should be fine, but my son and I are anything but happy. There is a feeling of emptiness and chaos inside us. We are on a journey away from a dark place towards a brighter horizon.

I had finally taken the massive step to leaving my destructive marriage in which I had been domestically abused for 25 years. Now my son and I found ourselves in unexplored territories."

My name is Johan Rylander. I'm 55 years old and live in Uppsala, Sweden. I was stuck in a destructive, toxic marriage for a quarter of a century. For 25 years, I had been one of the many invisible male victims of a female partner domestic abuse.

I want to share my story with you to raise awareness about this horrific violence that goes on daily, behind locked doors, all around the globe. Violence has no gender. The violence occurs where we are supposed to be most safe in our homes.

Of course, it's not possible for me to include everything that I experienced for 25 years in this one chapter. However, I aim to describe the different forms of abuse I was subjected to. It is essential to remember that intimate partner violence is much more than just physical abuse. We must also be aware that domestic violence can happen to anyone. For too long, people have believed that a perpetrator is a man, and that the victim is a woman. Another misperception regarding male domestic abuse victims is that he lives in a relationship where both partners subject each other to violence and that drugs and alcohol are involved.

I want to start by telling you a little bit about me.

How come I ended up in this abusive marriage? I, who had been privileged to be brought up in a calm, loving home full of warmth and respect. My parents taught me good values. They taught me the importance of standing up for what's right. Travelling down memory lane to my childhood, I see nothing but happiness and sunlight.

As a kid, I had a great interest in sports and music. I practised, became successful and competed in judo, badminton, and swimming. Aside from sports, I also enjoyed drawing and playing the piano. I worked as a tennis coach in my twenties and began competing in ballroom dancing.

My parents laid a solid and firm foundation on which I began building my life; as I reflect on my life's journey so far, it was a foundation that saved me from being destroyed by all those years of abuse. I never forgot who I am and how I was raised.

I met my wife through mutual friends. We soon became more than friends. Her Latin-American origin was only one of many things that attracted me. She was full of life, and her intensity inspired me. Despite our cultural differences, I noticed we shared similar interests. I felt I had met my soul mate. I was in seventh heaven. Had I only known what was to come.

Everything went so fast. I guess it's fair to say I was swept off my feet. It almost seemed too good to be true. Looking back, I now see multiple red flags, which I, at the time, was too blind to notice. She told me time and time again that I was the love of her life. She was very affectionate. She wanted to know everything about me. Already she had begun to talk about marriage and children.

How the psychological abuse began

Looking back on our first year together, I remember how my life changed. Things started to circle more and more around her. She wanted to spend every minute together. I didn't think so much of it then, but, with all facts in hand, it was there, and then the abuse began. As a couple living together, she started questioning my decisions and opinions. Doing things with my friends was suddenly something that led to discussions. She would get a headache or an anxiety attack. She would cry and ask me to stay at home with her instead. She made me feel sorry for her, so I gave in.

As an empath and sensitive person, I felt every little mood shift in her. What I didn't realize was that she had, already at this point, scanned me and knew exactly how to make me focus on her. Her well-being became my first and only priority. My interests, hobbies, and things I enjoyed suddenly didn't seem as important.

After one year together, we got married. But not in the way I had planned. We had decided to visit her family in her home country, and she made it very clear that we had to get married before going. She told me that her family would not accept us being unmarried. And as, by now, her desires had already begun to be our law, we got married. I remember the objections, especially from my mother. Having seen all the outbursts, mood shifts and how my wife-to-be was the one in charge of our relationship made my mother wonder if I was making the right decision in going through with the marriage.

We adopted her niece, an adorable little girl, at the same time our first son was born. Becoming a father was a dream coming true. There were so many things I had in mind that I wanted to do as a father. Sadly, it didn't turn out the way I wanted.

The psychological abuse took many different shapes. This form of abuse is very sophisticated. As a victim, you never know what your next day will look like. Little by little, my personality changed. I was always nervous and constantly walked on eggshells.

I turned into a master when it came to saying I was sorry. Even though I had done nothing wrong, by apologizing, I could make a situation get less terrible. Sadly, this was the advice I would give my kids when their mother was angry and blamed them for something they hadn't done. To apologize to her so that she would stop shouting at them. I remember how they looked at me, not understanding why they should apologize when they hadn't done anything wrong.

Coercive abuse

Her psychological and coercive abuse continued and became something I saw as usual. My days and my life were planned around her. This, of course, led to me being isolated from my parents and relatives. A sad and cruel contrast as my family is very dear to me. Having been able to share birthdays and holidays with my family, my wife had now made this impossible. She made me choose between her and my family. As I felt ashamed about this, I started making up reasons and lies as I explained to my parents and relatives why I had to stay at home.

My marriage didn't only affect my relationship with family and relatives. Soon I lost all my friends. I had been part of a quartet that played badminton every Friday evening. She forced me to stay at home. Once again, making me choose. I invented reasons why I couldn't join my friends, week after week. This led to them finding my replacement.

Her coercive abuse increased. Whenever a friend asked me if I wanted to do something, my standard answer would be, "I'll have to check. I'll get back to you". I felt it pointless to accept as I knew my wife would make a problem out of it. I didn't even bother to ask her as I already knew what she would say.

My fatherhood was also affected. I had always dreamt about being an active father who would take my kids out and play, practice sports or play games. As my wife demanded my full attention, being a father became a problem. Both my kids and I knew who was in charge. I noticed that whenever I told my kids to do something, they would turn their eyes towards their mother as she always had the last say.

Financial abuse

This coercive abuse also included our economy. She demanded complete control over our finances. I was forced to transfer my salary to her account. There was no point asking her how much we had in the account. She just told me I shouldn't bother and asked me at the same time why I didn't trust her.

It was awful not to have the slightest say regarding our economy. I could just quietly see her buying more and more things. Expensive stuff that we didn't need. This was her way of compensating for her depression. But it was also about creating a facade so that our friends would be impressed.

It was now that my financial trouble began. She prioritized all bills with her name. Bills with my name came last on her list, leading to me getting huge debts. My debts ended up with the bailiff. I'm still today, struggling with these debts.

Material abuse

She would use a very efficient tool from her abusive toolkit to keep me under control: to threaten to destroy my personal belongings. However, it didn't stop at threats. She destroyed the clothes and belongings I cared about, worth thousands and thousands of dollars. She broke five pairs of eyeglasses, and without eyeglasses, I couldn't see correctly. She took my wallet with my driver's license and other essential documents. To get my things back, one by one, I had to beg. I could notice how she enjoyed having power over me. I became smaller and smaller.

Physical abuse

Having been subjected to this psychological, coercive, economic, and material abuse for so long, I had become a pale shadow of myself. I didn't care about things. Nothing mattered. My life was about enduring from one day to the next. From having been an empathetic person, I had now developed emotional apathy.

As I, at this point, didn't care about the psychological abuse, she raised the bar. It was now that the physical abuse became her new ingredient. As a male victim of intimate partner violence, nobody believes you when you dare to tell the truth.

I remember when I finally had worked up my courage to go to the police after she had abused me physically. The first question they asked me was, "and what did you do first?". After that, I never contacted the police again.

Life became even worse when she passed this limit and started to use physical violence. I remember how I would think of my every move and my every word. It felt like I had turned into a little person. I felt ashamed to work with deep scratches on my face and arms. My colleagues asked me what I had done. I made up stories and told them I had been in the woods and scratched myself against branches.

Having our kids watch their mother physically abuse me was awful. I became good at foreseeing when things were heading towards physical violence and would flee out the door. I remember all those dark and ice-cold nights in wintertime when I had managed to escape and spent the nights in a freezing car. I did my best to spare my kids from witnessing physical violence. Also, I tried to explain that their mother was feeling bad and didn't mean to hit me. I did my best to comfort them and tell them I was okay.

Fleeing became my method of avoiding physical abuse. The police had warned me not to end up in situations where she subjected me to physical violence because the police, in nine cases out of ten, believed that it was the man who was the perpetrator of the violence.

Summary

After being denied help from social authorities several times during those long dark years, I got a break. They finally decided to help my son and me in my fifth attempt. I remember the feeling. Suddenly I was a free soul. It was like waking up from a 25-year-long sleep. Free from "that someone" who had been locking me inside a physical and mental prison for so long. Who had controlled my every step?

Here I was. With non-existing confidence. With a self-image which had turned to an all-time low. Having been so long in a small fishpond where I was familiar with every inch, I found myself in the middle of a big ocean with no clue about which direction to swim.

The awakening was brutal, and my tears were many when I, for the first time, began to understand why I had stayed so long and how I had normalized all the abnormalities that had been going on in my toxic and destructive marriage.

The journey back to everyday life and a new" me" commenced. But I have had to realize that it's going to take time. There will be pitfalls along the way. I never know what will trigger my

PTSD. I long for the day when I won't be reminded of her as I visit places she and I would go. I need to rely on friends and family who will play a significant and vital role as support and encouragement.

At 55, I finally enjoy being the father I always wanted to be. My kids are now 30, 26 and 17 years old. They are happy to have the opportunity to get to know their father. Now they see their father as he is. I receive phone calls from them for no particular reason. They want to talk. Life is sweet!

Today I'm head of a non-profit organization here in Sweden that helps male victims of domestic violence. I'm a Certified International Public Speaker and have made it my mission to raise awareness of domestic abuse. I'm also a Certified International Mindset and Empowerment Coach, helping men who have been victims of domestic violence to find their lost confidence.

Domestic violence has no gender, and no one should have to wait as long as 25 years to receive help. I hope that I'll be able to create a change so that all victims of domestic violence, no matter their gender or sexual orientation, are seen.

Now I'm a free man. Now I wake up every morning feeling alive. Now I'm the captain of my life. Now I'm in the driver's seat on my journey toward a new horizon! The journey hasn't been easy, BUT it has been worth every step so far!!!

Karen Ferguson

Author
Magazine Editor and Columnist
Public Speaker

Chapter 7

I REFUSED TO LET HIM WIN

By Karen Ferguson

I wonder when, or even if, these triggers will ever entirely stop. Will my mind and body stop suddenly reacting to perceived threats that, logically, I know are not threatening at all? Will I ever be comfortable knowing that I have enough money, or will I still pause in a moment of near panic when I have to spend money? I wonder if my need to be defensive, protective, and constantly on alert will ever really leave me and, more importantly to me, will I ever truly feel safe again?

It's funny, you know, when it comes to abuse, there is often this perception that once you leave your abuser, or once they move out of your home, it is over, and you can "move on" or "forget it". Now I can't, and would never presume to, speak for everyone, but try as I might, and I do admit here that I am very hard on myself when this happens; I cannot just move on or forget it. Not because I spend my days wallowing or pitying myself. I've never done that, not even on my worst days, but because smells, sounds, loud noises, situations, and venues can trigger some fear that leaves me shaking or feeling sick. I can be left almost breathless at the enormity of what I endured and survived.

I can't always identify the trigger and know that that is not uncommon with PTSD, but it can still floor me. It can leave me feeling shaken, on edge, and reluctant to go out, or stay in. It can leave me in desperate need of someone to be there with me and yet a desire never to be or feel vulnerable with anyone again. I find it hard to trust people, and the idea that I might need to ask for help or show certain emotions in front of others is often just too much to cope with.

I know people have told me they are here for me, and I genuinely appreciate it. Still, the thing is, not only do most people not get it, not understand how it could feel to have experienced prolonged abuse from someone who promised to love them forever, but I don't always know how to explain myself and how I feel.

People often offer platitudes and comments like "Let's hope…" I'm sure they are doing what they feel is right, but I don't want or need this. I don't want or need yet another person telling me what I should think or do. I don't want my fear dismissed with logic; I want it acknowledged.

If you asked me today why I am telling you about the after-effects of abuse rather than the abuse itself, it's because you can find my whole story in my book, *My Life with A Sociopath. It Can Happen to Anyone*, and secondly, what happens after the abuse stops, is almost worse than the abuse itself.

I found myself in the supermarket with my son, gripping the trolley and desperately trying to control my breathing because panic had taken hold of me. I went through periods where I would shake for days at a time, not large noticeable shakes, but enough to exhaust me. I've smelt him in my house when there was no possible way he could be there, and I've seen him several times, despite that being impossible. He has been in my dreams, where I can't escape him. It's like having an invisible enemy that dogs your every move, and this made me so frustrated and angry at times because I felt like he kept winning, that no matter what I did, I couldn't shake him fully from my life.

What did he do to cause this trauma within me? He lied, punched things, broke things, smashed in two front doors, held his fist just inches from my face, refused to speak to me for days, and looked at me with venom, such a pure hatred that I never thought possible.

He told me that he loved me, hated me, couldn't live without me, hoped I'd die, was his everything, hoped my cancer returned, was his soul mate, and had planned my murder. He stole from my purse and bank account and went through my possessions to find and steal money I had been forced to hide. He pushed us into debt, nearly costing us our house, spent money he didn't have and left me to pay off his debts. He was aggressive, violent, controlling and a borderline alcoholic (he certainly drank every day). He would cause arguments for no reason and throw his dinner in the garbage if someone looked at him "funny" or if they didn't praise his cooking enough. He stalked me, called me vile names, tried to use my children against me, wished me dead, used threats of suicide, swallowed pills and alcohol in front of me, harassed me in person, by phone and with messages, and threatened to shoot me and drove his car into my house.

Some of his actual messages, all sent in one evening: -

19:07 BLOCK ME BECAUSE I TAKE IT TO SEND YOU MESSAGES IS ABUSE AS IT THEN GETS ME ARRESTED.
19:10 AND NOT REPLYING IT ALL I NEED TO KNOW I HOPE YOU HAVE A WONDERFUL LIFE
19:20 GOODBYE, I DID LOVE YOU.
19:31 I'M NOT SORRY ABOUT THE MESS; YOU WILL HAVE TO CLEAN IT UP.
19:35 I WON'T BE HERE TOMORROW.

19:54 AND SORRY TO SAY THIS, YOU TOLD ME YOU NEVER WANTED TO BE LIKE YOUR MUM; YOU HAVE TURNED INTO HER.

19:59 YOU MAY BE SORRY WILL GET A FEW TEXTS WITH SOME HOME TRUTHS, BUT I DON'T CARE NOW BECAUSE I KNOW YOU WON'T CARE, OR BEST STILL, I WON'T BE THERE, AND YOU WILL HAVE TO DEAL WITH IT.

20:00 I AM GOING TO MAKE (OUR DAUGHTER) THE LAST EVER PUDDING I DO FOR HER. I HOPE THAT MAKES YOU HAPPY.

20:07 GIN VODKA AND WINE MAKE A GOOD COCKTAIL.

20:09 AT LEAST YOU CAN KEEP ALL THESE TO BUILD YOUR CASE UP.

20:11 SO THIS IS WHY I'M HAPPY TO TEXT YOU ALL NIGHT UNTIL THE END.

20:12 AND IT'S OK. I HAVE DELETED EVERYTHING FROM MY PHONE.

20:13 I HOPE YOU ARE ENJOYING THIS.

20:13 SORRY HOPE

20:14 BECAUSE, TO BE HONEST, I AM YOUR LISP.

20:14 LOSS

20:19 AND YET AGAIN, I'M NOT BEING BULLYING. I'VE JUST HAD ENOUGH OF EVERYTHING, AND NOW IT'S TIME.

20:20 I'VE DONE OR NOT DONE MY BEST WHATEVER I CAN'T DO ANYMORE.

20:20 I HOPE YOU ARE ENJOYING THIS.

20:21 NO RESPONSE MEANS YOU ARE.

20:27 I HOPE YOU ARE ENJOYING THIS.

20:30 AND TO BE HONEST, I DO NOT THINK BUT KNOW YOU ARE.

20:33 COME ON, GIVE ME SOME RESPONSE; IT WILL HELP ME EVEN MORE IF YOU DON'T WANT TO THEN ON YOUR CONSCIENCE BE IT NOT MINE.

20:40 OK, YOU WIN AGAIN. I HATE YOU. I HATE LIFE WITHOUT YOU, SO I'M GOING TO BE NASTY NOW HOPE YOUR CANCER COMES BACK, AND YOU HAVE NOBODY TO LOOK AFTER YOU. I DON'T CARE ANYMORE, NOT ABOUT YOU OR OUR CHILDREN; THEY CAN SURVIVE; YOU HAVE KILLED ME.

20:41 AS I SAID, EVERYBODY LOSES NOW.

20:43 YOU GET NOTHING; THEY GET NOTHING; YOU GET THE MESS TO CLEAN UP GOODBYE.

He was arrested the next day after having sent a total of 42 messages, called 11 times, and left three voicemails in just under 24 hours, despite me telling him clearly to stop.

The system didn't help either because it just didn't feel supportive. Instead, it felt disjointed, confusing, difficult to navigate, and, if I'm honest, so very intrusive.

Everything seems so weighted in favour of the perpetrator that I can truly understand why people stay or why they return. Simply put, it is such hard work to navigate this system, so soul-destroying to have to tell your story time and time again to get help, and I am not exaggerating when I say that every step of the journey can and often does re-traumatise you.

My ex held up my divorce by refusing to acknowledge receipt of the documents, so I had no choice but to pay a specialist to serve him. The ridiculous thing is, he was in prison at the time, so given that the papers had to be delivered via them, and they had to serve him, why wasn't that enough? I was told that the judge wouldn't move forward with the divorce unless he acknowledged them. The system kept me married to this man longer than necessary.

There has been so much confusion for me, trying to work out what to do, who to speak to and what help is available. It might seem a bit mad, but when people told me to ask if I needed anything, I was at a bit of a loss. I didn't know what I needed for the simple reason that I had never been here before. And the truth is, I doubt that I could have been given the things I needed the most at that moment because I mostly needed to feel safe, and I didn't. I needed to stop being forced to talk about it. I wanted to know that I could afford to look after my children and have a home.

It barely seemed any time between the day he was arrested and the day he was due to be released. There was little respite between statements, court appearances, agency referrals, safety assessments, trying to find a divorce solicitor, applications for Legal Aid, fighting red tape, sorting out finances, paying off his debts, fighting to get help, him breaching his restraining order, more police investigations, having the front of my house rebuilt, creating exclusion zones, having to tell yet more people about my private life to protect my children and everything else I had to deal with before he was out again.

The injustices of this system meant that he still had rights even though he could have killed my daughter. To protect my child from a man she doesn't want to see, I would have to put her through giving statements and months of interviews with strangers. There would be court appearances, where I would have to tell my story, again and again, provide more statements, and probably face him and who knows what else. All this is something I would do in a heartbeat to protect my child, but why should I have to?

Why does a man, who told me he wouldn't leave just me or him behind, refuses to pay anything towards his children, tried to extort money from me, and who could have killed my child still have rights? Why does my child have to be traumatised yet again to stop this man from seeing her? Why is it left to the survivor, the traumatised victim of abuse, to fight the system? Why doesn't the system work to protect us and work more seamlessly to help us?

Until it does, no survivor will be adequately protected.

I still don't understand it, you know. I don't get why he decided to take this particular path. He chose aggression over a discussion, control over compassion and destruction over everything else. He could have accepted it had ended, stayed a part of his children's lives, and remained a part of the family. Instead, he chose to destroy his future. Yes, I mean his future, not mine, because I have one. I will love again; I still have my children, and I still have room to grow.

He has made his life so much harder than it needed to be. But he won't ever take responsibility for this. It will always be my fault where he is concerned, and I guess therein lies my only worry. How far will he take his sense of blame against me? Will he seek to cause further damage, or will he walk away?

It's a challenging place to be because I don't know; what I do know, though, is that I will not give him one more minute of my thought, not one more ounce of my feelings, and I will not let him blacken my heart.

What is my life like now? Perhaps a better question would be; was it worth it, was the pain and hassle worth getting him out of my everyday life? Yes, 100%, absolutely worth it.

Could it have been made easier by the system? Again, yes, it could, but despite moments of doubt, moments of wondering if I wouldn't have been better off just staying, just putting up with it, I know I did the right thing in ending it.

As a co-author of this book, my story, *My Life With A Sociopath - It Can Happen to Anyone,* was released in May 2022. I have also written *Passion, Pain and No Promises. Confusion, Control and Conditioning, and Who Am I?*

I run a growing number of workshops designed to help women build confidence and use the power of writing to deal with trauma; I'm a Global Ambassador for Stand Up Survivor, I run a vlog series called *Life Chat with Karen and Alex* and continue to raise my voice as much as I can to help educate others about abuse and support those who cannot speak for themselves.

If I could change one thing, it would be that education on domestic abuse is spread and created by survivors, not from theoretical evidence assessed and interpreted by those who have never experienced abuse. Give us a real voice, and we will show you how we can make a change for the better.

Do I like who I am now? Yes, I do. More accurately, I love who I am now, and I will continue to love the person I am, evolving into a woman who is bold, brave, confident, and a force to be reckoned with.

Karen Ward

Holistic Wellness and Mindset
Transformation Coach
Founder of Joi Luck Club

Chapter 8

LETTING GO OF THE PAIN

By Karen Ward

If I can help one victim with my story, sharing my pain will be worthwhile, helping another individual, have the strength to leave and have hope for a better life.

I constantly reminded myself of one thing since my traumatic experiences began: there is ALWAYS hope.

Nightmares still creep in every so often, of the fear I experienced every day while I was married. It is not an easy experience to navigate through, but it takes time. Trying to feel "worthy" of anything takes time after the abuser has taken that from you. Even feeling "worthy" enough to have one's photo taken is a huge hurdle to overcome. Being drained by an abuser of many things in your life it is a lifelong process to regain and overcome in some capacity. It is a process of regaining hope. It is a process of recovering identity in oneself.

It is a process of regaining faith in people as well. Trusting others is a process for victims of abuse. Many individuals think that domestic violence is something you "get over."

It is far from it. It is something a victim/survivor deals with as best as they can every day. Every domestic violence victim has their unique experience, but all are horrific, whatever the experience. I was very naïve about how the system works, as I was never expecting to have to deal with, nor be married into, an abusive situation. Who am I to those well connected or to the "power Players" in the system?! I have learned that they consider me as nothing. They still think of me as nothing and not important enough to listen to. Unfortunately, in our county system, most women are considered insignificant and disposable unless they have money and connections to powerful men.

There are many facets and paths which an individual surviving domestic violence must take and often is forced to endure. For me, overcoming domestic violence was only the beginning of my path and journey through a corrupt system and learning and uncovering the "mafia-type" entanglements of the various individuals and entities of the pay-to-play mentality and practices in Will County and beyond.

Toxicity abounds throughout the system, and multiple entities, including some police departments, are and have been, engulfed with many abusive officers and those that aid and enable them.

Their lack of accountability and failure to follow the rules/laws, especially when it comes to domestic violence/police perpetrated domestic violence, and address the system's corrupt behaviors, only leads victims to distrust the system further, and many choose to stay in their abusive situations due to hearing of others traumatic experiences like mine. Why would many women leave when the system doesn't care and doesn't believe "in justice for all." Only for the well connected with money to pay. In my situation, some attorneys were filled with greed and lust for money and power, making them take unethical and illegal paths from the beginning.

Unfortunately, the system and those that have created it, starting with the legislature in our nation and state and its higher courts and beyond, are not interested in addressing the problems. Corruption encompasses our courts, and law enforcement, and the entire system fails victims of domestic violence and sexual assault every day. The only ones truly there for victims are DV and underfunded SA agencies. The legislators that think they "provide enough" are uneducated regarding these issues and those surrounding them. Victims and Survivors are being pushed aside by the system rulers. Anyone who has not walked through traumas like domestic violence and sexual assault cannot begin to speak of the added pain caused by a system that makes it abundantly worse through their ignorance and disregard for victims/survivors.

One of the worst moments (and there were so many) during the end of the long extensive divorce process, after I escaped, was not only the fact that my attorney did not have my best interests at all (and I was naïve to think he did), but the fact that my attorney told me that the system, "Doesn't care about the truth of domestic violence nor what happened to me", but "only cares about what they choose to happen" with the outcome, and who they choose to win. It is their game based on money and connections. I was also told the decision was made before anything started within the court years earlier. Wasted time by a system that consistently fails women, especially those married to wealthy and well-connected men and those with power.

The system failed me and continues to do so. This was also on a day that the system tore two children away from a loving mother and allowed an abuser to further alienate the children from their loving mother because there is no accountability or following of the rules for the well connected. But as all survivors, especially mothers, are well aware , their abuser will stop at nothing to further hurt them, primarily through the children they share.

The system fails victims/survivors, especially those married to the well-connected, and especially those married to police officers, who abuse their police powers, which the system and their departments allow them to.

Those in the system, including attorneys, therapists, "experts", etc. that are not willing to do the right thing and step up for victims of domestic violence and sexual assault should not be in the field., The same for judges, especially when they have no regard for victims but instead only their agendas and pocketbooks.

Sadly, when victim's advocates from the County States Attorney's office and various legislators' offices repeat what I heard many times, including from my second attorney; "You won't win anything because of who your spouse is related to, their extensive wealth and who they know", you feel alone, as I have. Unfortunately, attorneys, judges, doctors/therapists, politicians, and law enforcement displayed unethical behaviours throughout the process.

Gas lighting by strangers and relatives alike towards victims/survivors of domestic violence only enables the abuser to further victimize the survivor, both within the community and the system.

Being "Gaslit" by family members and others makes the traumatic experience of domestic violence and sexual assault even more complicated, with those individuals not choosing to know the truth. Still, the false narrative they create makes the situation more comfortable for them, especially within their lifestyle.

A toxic court system environment, especially within the courthouse itself, and police departments supposed to serve all, have become increasingly corrupt and harmful for victims/survivors.

I remember these words to this day…of something inside me, saying to me and reminding me that "there is always hope." Even in the darkest days of the abuse I endured. Especially after the most traumatic occasions, such as when I was pregnant with our first child and was pushed down the stairs as I was getting ready for work. He yelled, that "if I lost it (the baby), he wouldn't give me another one", Even then, I still held on to hope.

His behavior escalated after he became a police officer, as he was taught how to lie, play the system and utilize his connections even more to get his way.

This was further enabled by his well-connected union family and their political, judicial and union friends. Sadly, the system enables abusers, especially police officers, to further abuse, escalating power and control.

PPDV (Police-Perpetrated Domestic Violence) is very much ignored in Illinois and the United States of America.

Many judicial officials, legislators and others don't take this problem seriously and ignore calls to reform the system.

Yeah, I have learned why they wouldn't take it seriously as a problem when the "problem" and "games" they have set up have worked in their favor, as they had planned.

Sadly, society thinks that domestic violence is only one definition/one example of a situation. Still, it is many horrible situations that victims have to deal with by their abusers.

Ignorance of the real-world traumatic experiences that domestic violence victims must face is a way for enablers and those that ignore and further hurt victims to continue the uneducated mentality towards domestic violence victims and the issue/epidemic of domestic violence.

I not only deal with physical, emotional/mental and financial abuse by my perpetrator, but the system further traumatized me through their forms of abuse, including but not limited to; Sexual

Assault by a court official and emotional/mental abuse by other officials in the courts, because they can. Power, Greed, Personal Agendas, money and control are the themes of many of the "players" in the system, and my divorce trial attorney told me that it is "all a game" and they don't care about the truth of what happens to victims. My divorce attorney manipulated me the entire time and forced me to drop my OP (Order of Protection) at the beginning of the process, which only escalated their "game" and my perpetrators' abusive behavior.

The sexual assault by the "court official/expert" was ignored by hundreds of thousands of women, undoubtedly, for decades- because of his connections to the "players" in the system. I was told not to tell of my assault by my former attorney, and was further shamed and bullied into keeping quiet by members of the system that had known about his criminal behaviors for many years.

The opposing counsel admitted to being aware of this abuse that caused added trauma to victims like myself. But there was no change to the system. No deep investigation was done, and for the damage the court official did, the consequences did not fit the crimes committed.

This was because of his connections, both within the court system with the judges and with the legislative ties. To the system, victims were just another piece of garbage they considered/consider unimportant. Each victim that this "court official" sexually assaulted matters and should have never been shamed, as I was, by my attorney and his pals in the system, for decades.

I have learned that these things happen in the county where I live, but nothing is done to change it, as these players choose how their "game" is played. State reps, Senators, County Executives and their offices, as well as many attorneys and judges, guardian-ad-items and "court experts" come on board as long as their price is right.

Creating the needed change is a much more difficult task than I thought. As I have been told, I need to "be at peace" with what happened and not "rock the boat" because no one cares. I care.

I care about the millions of others following that have yet to escape. Those that are not listened to, are ridiculed, made fun of, and mocked. Not only by their abuser and the system, but also many times by family members that have no idea about anything involving abuse and are uneducated in the many levels and kinds of abuse that occur daily in the lives of so many individuals in this country and world. Each victim's voice matters. Not just mine, but every victim's voice. Every voice has hope. Some victims' voices are silenced by their abusers, but they are still heard because of what they have endured.

Always have hope, and never stop letting your voice be heard because you are not alone. I always forgive, but my voice will not be silenced. I will help change the system and help other victims not go through the same traumas I have faced.

I will continue to work to seek changes in a system that refuses to acknowledge there are huge problems with corruption, pay-to-play, and further victimizing victims / survivors of domestic violence and sexual assault.

Kindness and Caring for each other matter.
I know I am Stronger, and I Am Worthy. I remember who I am and who I want to be.

I Forgive.
Always.
I Have Hope.
Always.

Leda Watts

Author
Advocate for Gun Violence &
Domestic Abuse
Public Speaker

Chapter 9

HOW DID I GET HERE?

By Leda Watts

Robbed of My Innocence

As I sit and reflect on my life, I am struck by how much hurt and pain I have endured. I contemplate how I got here and when it all began.

It was 1982, and Toledo, Ohio, was the setting. I was ten years old when I went to my great uncle's house for the final family gathering for my great aunt, who was dying of cancer. My 23-year-old cousin followed me upstairs to the bathroom and molested me. He warned me not to tell anyone. I recall feeling scared, dirty, and ashamed. A few weeks later, after my aunt died, we went to the funeral. Family and friends attended the repast at my grandmother's house.

With everyone downstairs, that same cousin came upstairs to find me playing with my cousin and my grandmother's neighbor. She was eight years old. My cousin left the room because he had previously molested her, and she was afraid to be near him. That left my grandmother's neighbor and me vulnerable to him.

As my grandmother's neighbor and I were sitting side-by-side on one of the twin beds, it happened again. The sense of being terrified, humiliated, and filthy had returned to me. He came after me first. He tried putting his tongue in my mouth and on my face. I was squirming, trying to get away from him. He put his hand in my underwear and his fingers inside my vagina.

My neighbor was crying and didn't know what to do. He pinned her down by holding her throat with his other hand. She was able to break free. I was able to get away from him as well. My neighbor went downstairs crying, and I was right behind her. My grandmother asked her what had happened. She said she wanted to go home. She didn't say anything more and returned to her home. My grandmother didn't probe to find out what happened.

Shhh…

I had a dark secret that I couldn't reveal. At the age of ten, I was enraged and despised myself. On my shoulders was the weight of the entire universe. I was perplexed, and I couldn't figure out why. I recall thinking it was my fault, and despite growing up in a house full of people and family, I always felt alone because of an ugly little secret I kept hidden that impacted every part of my life.

Keeping My Baby

I became a teenage mother to a beautiful little boy when I was 16 years old, and I fell in love with him the moment I saw him. I recall holding him in my arms and telling him that mommy would never allow anyone to hurt him.

Even though my parents and family adored my child, I had brought disappointment and disgrace to my family by becoming a teenage mother and being talked about and chastised for it. It brought up painful memories of a dark secret I'd kept hidden for so long, which made me feel useless and miserable. It caused me not to always make the best decisions.

My First Marriage…I wasn't ready!

I married at 18 to try to prove my worth and erase the embarrassment I had caused my family by producing a child out of wedlock. Still, my expectations about marriage and how things should be were radically different from my husband's. Our marriage began with difficulties, and we didn't receive much support since others believed we were too young. Outside of the marriage, there was a lot of interference from his family and friends, who thought he should be sowing his oats instead of marrying, and from my family, who didn't care for him.

And the fact that I had sex issues didn't help matters.

Sex was not something I liked or enjoyed. Being touched bothered me. I'd always have the feeling of being humiliated and filthy.

He eventually became involved with the wrong crowd, and his lifestyle shifted, which was not in our family's best interests. He decided to become a drug dealer and a ladies' man. He was arrogant and self-centered. He did not support our children or me financially. To him, our union was inconsequential. He purposefully proceeded to harm me through his deception and dishonesty. He did not physically abuse me, but he did mentally. I was naïve and unfamiliar with the streets.

He Set Me Up!

He approached me one day with an older woman he introduced to me as his uncle's girlfriend. He stated that she owed him money but had misplaced her identification and that she would have the person who employed her write a check in my name to cash so she could pay him. I was completely unaware of what was going on. They returned a few hours later with a check and drove me to the bank.

I went in to complete the transaction, but instead, I was handcuffed, arrested, and taken to jail. My husband was nowhere to be found. He had fled the scene leaving me alone to handle this situation. I was seven months pregnant and facing uttering and publishing charges (check fraud).

When I bonded out, his only concern was whether I had provided the police with his or the lady's name. That should have ended our marriage at that point, but I stayed, and things just got worse.

Nothing changed

His actions on the streets nearly invariably manifested themselves on my doorstep. Especially the drama of his many entanglements with different women. This ranged from them calling to tell me to check my vehicle for used condoms from the night before, to me returning home from work early and finding him naked in our bed with the neighbor with our children in the next room. And learning that she was pregnant with his child, whilst I was pregnant with our last child. I didn't want to feel like a failure, so I stayed. My marriage was a disaster for me.

Close to Death

One morning, I awoke with agonizing back pain. My skin was heated and sweaty, but I was freezing. I couldn't walk. I was taken to the hospital and admitted. My kidneys were both severely infected. I had a 104-degree fever that wouldn't go away. They used cold blankets on me and gave me antibiotics that did not work. The doctors had asked the Chaplain to come in and pray with me because they didn't think I'd make it. My fever had finally broken, but I wasn't yet out of the woods. I had spent many days in the hospital. My husband had been absent since the moment I was admitted.

After watching a news story from my hospital bed, I signed out of the hospital against medical advice. The cops were stopped by the neighborhood crack addict at the chicken restaurant down the street from my house. He told them he had murdered his wife and locked her in their bedroom while getting high and going back and forth, babysitting my small children in our home. I couldn't understand how my husband could endanger our children by leaving them in the care of a crack addict.

I Have to Save Me & My Children
I took my children and left our house. I filed for divorce after eight years of marriage. I didn't want anything to do with him anymore. He had begun to follow me.

One night, I awoke with a knife to my throat. He had climbed through the window on the third floor of my apartment. My son bolted from the apartment, startling the neighbors. They came to my aid. I was grateful, but even that came at a cost.

Can't Trust Anyone

That neighbor eventually came to take advantage of the situation.

He asked me to rent him a professional karaoke system from a music store for a party.

I agreed and signed my name to the rental agreement. You'd think that after the check incident, I'd learned my lesson. I made a wrong decision. He didn't return the equipment to the music store. I was arrested and charged with larceny by conversion (failure to return rental property). I was unable to make bond. Instead, I fought the charge in court from jail from December to March.

I was sentenced and charged with a felony. I was released in March and placed on one-year probation. My self-esteem was shattered even further. My divorce had been finalized. Shortly after that, my ex went to prison for murder.

The Devil Wasn't Finished with Me

I met the father of my two younger children. My first impression of him was that he possessed positive characteristics. He had a friendly smile, good communication skills, and appeared to be a good listener. He was amusing and would occasionally compliment me. I would tell him everything that had happened to me. He would say to me about his life, his relationship with his mother, and his experiences. He turned out to be just as broken as I was. He was revealed to be a true Dr Jekyll and Mr. Hyde.

Everything I told him about my life he turned around and used against me. My desire to be in a loving relationship was solely mine, as he lacked a loving relationship with his mother. He had no idea how to project and express love to a woman. He had a deep-seated hatred for women, and I paid the price.

He would blame me for all his problems. He was a heavy drinker. What I thought was just marijuana turned out to be cocaine. He terrified my children and me. He was psychologically, physically, emotionally, and verbally abusive to me. He would have deceptive thoughts and accuse me of things that were not true. I can't recall ever being happy in the relationship. He complained daily.

My Angel in Disguise
Tracy, my first cousin, who is more like a sister to me, was a great source of encouragement for me. She was unaware of the full scope of what was going on. She had a sneaking suspicion it was more.

Not only was I embarrassed to tell her what was going on, but it was also the only time I could escape my fears. I felt normal when I was laughing and talking with her, but I fell deeper into depression when she left.

Constant Fear, Shame & Humiliation

He would harass me about my friends and family until I isolated myself from them to avoid confusion. He would become enraged and assault me because I had children with my first husband. He would constantly tell me how unimportant and unattractive I was. He would insult me, tell me I was stupid, and that no other man would want me with children. Over 15 years, I went to the ER frequently and made up many lies about what happened.

He had threatened to kill me on numerous occasions. His abuse continued. He would frequently blacken my eyes, break my fingers with pliers, and beat me with beer bottles and belts. He said he was tired of using his fist as he continued slamming my head into the wall. My injuries were treated at the hospital. I ended up with 15 staples in the top of my skull.

He would wreck my home, destroying furniture, cars, and other personal items. I had to replace these items regularly, causing financial stress and feeling stuck with no way out.

Finally, a Friend

Jamil Muhammad, a gentleman from outside of Baltimore, befriended me and expressed compassion and understanding for my situation without passing judgment. He loved me and treated me with integrity. He spiritually uplifted me, acknowledged my fears, and assisted in breaking my children's father's mental grip on me. He has remained a good friend to me.

God Had Other Ideas

I assured myself that I would never get into another relationship and would be perfectly content single as time passed. Gregory Watts, my soulmate, and life companion, was sent by him. For the second time, I married.

In my husband, I found everything that I had ever imagined love to be. His strength, humility, and sensitivity for others fascinate me. He is dependable, a good provider, and a suitable guardian. He loves my children and me unconditionally, which has helped me develop self-esteem and confidence in myself in the safe, caring environment he has built for us.

In my life, he has brought me calm, contentment, and stability.

My heart was shattered on April 9, 2017

After everything I'd been through, I believed I'd finally arrived at a point in my life where I felt fulfilled. My five boys and two girls, as well as myself, were content. We were excited about our new future, and our view on life had improved significantly. We had a close-knit family, but it was only for a brief time.

Louis, 28, and Alex, 24, were leaving their grandparents' house to see acquaintances around the corner. Two older males, freshly released from prison, approached them as they walked to their friends' home. Louis was shot eight times and Alex five times in an execution-style shooting.

Those injuries caused their death. My innocent sons were executed because of retaliation for the wrongdoings of their father and his family.

Who were Louis & Alex?

They attended college.

Louis worked at the Chrysler plant, wrote music, acted, was a natural comedian, and multi-talented person. He volunteered at a senior living facility.

Alex had Asperger's syndrome, which is a form of autism. He was a true artist who could draw in 3D. He was learning carpentry.

Both fathers were involved in their children's lives and adored them. They were active members of their community.

I struggle with the pain and anger of losing them daily, but I am coping thanks to prayer and the continued love and support of my husband, family, My FOCUS LLC, and Mildred Muhammad.

Summary
I am now an advocate for gun control and domestic violence. I'm a well-known professional speaker on gun violence and domestic violence.

I've given talks in communities to increase awareness. Gun violence is a persistent problem that appears to have a global reach. Understanding the dynamics of this topic, as well as how fragmented our globe is, makes reaching a logical decision challenging.

Every day, the news reports on individuals or groups of people being shot or murdered. Each case is unique. I will continue to raise awareness about this problem. Guns, legal or illegal, are present in our homes. Nobody knows when or if they will be shot or killed by a child or an adult with a gun.

Domestic violence is still a global problem. Another societal concern that we continue to brush off. Working together, we must take steps to establish safe environments for our children and their children.

Rene' Michelle

Best Selling Author
Advocate against Domestic
Violence and Sexual Abuse
CEO/Founder of Pain Purpose

Chapter 10

THE LITTLE GIRL WHO WAS SILENCED

By René Michelle

The little girl who was silenced has finally found her voice!

As I sit and think about the things I've endured and the trauma I have overcome, I can honestly say "But God- a little girl shouldn't know anything about sexual intercourse", and yet I did!

As early as five, I remember being touched and fondled by several family members. I thought it was normal behavior. How would I have known otherwise?

Mom wasn't present, and even when she was, she was ducking and dodging the right hooks that daddy was serving her; even when she was present if you get my drift, she wasn't. I was the fourth child out of five and was always regularly told, OMG (She-gene), which is my nickname, go sit down somewhere. As a young child, I was constantly being silenced, so throughout my life, I always made it my business to ensure I was heard!

In the beginning, I was this quiet, shy, naive young girl. Who wanted and needed attention. It felt like no one paid any attention to me except daddy. I searched for that kind of love and someone that could give it to me. Someone, anyone, to love me as my daddy did.

Daddy wasn't the best husband, but he was a great father. He showed his kids, all of us, especially me being the baby girl, so much love. There's no way I can blame Mom for not being present because taking care of five children, keeping house, and being a wife wasn't the easiest task, especially under the circumstances she had to deal with, with the abuse and all.

Through all the hectic nights of screaming, yelling and glass breaking, I would lay in my bed and fantasize about being somewhere else. I would wonder if other kids dealt with what I was dealing with. Over time, the beatings got so bad that grandma would have to come over and take care of us because Mom was hospitalized for weeks due to the abuse.

While she was gone, daddy would bring tutors to the house, as he called them, and I think they were doing more tutoring for him than us. We never had an opportunity to interact with them, for they would come through, handle their business with daddy and leave.

As I look back, it makes me feel sickened to know that grown-ups don't have the sense to realize kids don't stay kids forever. We do eventually grow up. What was he thinking?

Time moved on, but the beatings continued and finally, thank you Jesus, Mom removed us from that situation. For me, it was bittersweet. Despite my feelings about leaving my dad, a part of me was happy that my Mom would finally be free from his abuse. She waited until he went to work, took the five of us, and ran to my grandfather's house, many miles away from home.

We eventually got settled there, and as time passed, Mom got a job. One day, we were left in my aunt's care, my mother's sister's. As we played in my grandpa's house yard, a car pulled up; surprisingly, it was my daddy. He ordered us to get into the car. He said that Mom told him he could come to get us. Everyone else looked concerned, but I was happy to see my daddy again finally. We all jumped in the car, and he drove off.

We eventually found out daddy had kidnapped us and that he told my Mom that she had to come back home if she ever wanted to see us again. She was working, and some time passed, but she eventually decided to return home despite how she may have felt about doing so.

She knew things would likely be as they were before we left. She was so right. The beatings began again, and at that point, Mom had honestly had enough, and she took us again and ran.

This time we went to a Domestic Violence Shelter for women in Washington DC. No one could know who we were, as we had to hide our identity. It was terrifying for me. We had never been to a big city before, so it was somewhat intimidating. We saw huge rats and stray cats for the very first time. The kids there were so mean I just wanted to go home and be with my friends and family and what we were used to. It was very traumatizing. However, not as traumatizing as hearing the beatings from the next room. Despite that, I would ask Mom when we would go home every day, and she would reply tomorrow.

Me being a child at the time, I didn't understand. Tomorrow would never come, but I was happy. Mom left dad because he wasn't suitable for her, and no one deserves the way he treated her. On the other hand, he treated his kids well; it was a confusing time for me.

Whilst staying at the shelter, I would sit in school and daydream about being home with my dad and the friends I grew up with.

Some would say it was selfish, but I was a child and didn't know any better. It felt good to have peace of mind, so it was a blessing that Mom removed herself from that situation.

In the end, I felt lost because the one person that ever showed me genuine love I couldn't talk to or see, or possibly ever speak to again. My heart was torn. Happy for my Mom but sad for me. I felt a void. I was back to being told to sit down somewhere and not having a voice.

In time I found my voice and would never be silenced again. I had endured sexual abuse throughout my life, and it seemed to get worse once we left Dad. Being away from him made me more of a target for these things.

I was raped at the age of 11 by some guy who was a family friend. It happened again when I was 14 when I was finally able to visit my daddy for the first time since the divorce. Similarly, at the age of 26, I was raped by a so-called friend. I have been through so much turmoil one would think that I would or should be an angry, bitter woman; I'm the complete opposite!

Growing up, anyone who knew me would never have imagined I had endured what I had. I was always making people laugh and trying to make people happy. Looking back at it, I was laughing in order not to cry.

I dealt with rape and molestation most of my life. Although this was not anything new to me, it was still harrowing. It was a little different because, this time, strangers were doing these things to me, not family. I felt that what was happening to me wasn't right or normal for the first time. I didn't know that the sexual abuse I had been enduring wasn't normal. After all, I had been trained at a very young age that I couldn't tell anyone because I would get in trouble, and it was our little secret.

I finally decided to no longer allow anyone else to touch me without my consent. I eventually moved to Philadelphia. My Mom remarried, and we finally had some normality in our lives.

I met my first love and decided I wanted to have a sexual relationship on my terms for the first time in my life. I was in control, and nobody would ever touch me again without my consent.

I had two children and ended up back in DC, Md Va area., which led me to the relationship that would change my life forever. I met a gentleman, and that was precisely what he was when we met. He did everything for me, like holding the door open and everything a gentleman does for a lady. He did all of that. He was so handsome and sweet.

It wasn't what it seemed, and he started showing another side of him. He became very violent, beating me so severely that I suffered from a Grand Mall epileptic seizure due to head trauma.

I had to run for my life. During this time, I discovered that I was blessed with my 3rd blessing, my baby girl. Yes, I was pregnant by him, and we have a beautiful daughter that we created.

Despite what life throws your way, you have the option to turn lemons into lemonade. I chose to take all my pain and turn it into my purpose, which, by the way, is the name of my non-profit. It helps women and children who are displaced due to domestic violence. I am now a national advocate against domestic violence and sexual assault and a best-selling author. I have shared my story at the delegates' house to help get bills passed against domestic violence.

Please, whatever you do, never let your past trauma dictate your future! I am now a radio show host for my podcast, René Michelle Unstuck. I'm an Ambassador for Raw Beauty, another non-profit that works with and supports women who have overcome domestic violence and also raises awareness around breast cancer.

I've been honored with numerous awards over the years, and the one that means the most to me is the I'M STILL STANDING AWARD from my mentor Ms Mildred Muhammad, whom I thank for this opportunity and who I hold in very high regard.

The world became a better place the day I decided not to allow anyone to silence me anymore. My journey of being unmuted started in 2012, and I'm still standing and fighting to help others come out of the darkness. Won't you stand with me? Forgiveness is necessary. As I was finding my truth, I found out and am now dealing with the death of my daughter's father. Despite what we endured, my daughter is broken because of his death. I'm thankful I came to forgive him for all he had done to me, allowing me to find peace.

RIP. I wish for my daughter's sake and granddaughter and the rest of his kids and grandkids that he could have received the help he needed while he was here.

Forgiveness is about healing and helping yourself as well as others too. Thanks to my Mom for giving me life and for the sacrifices she made.

Thanks to my kids for saving my life.

Tynia Canada

Founder of Inspirational Spirit of
the Phoenix Inc.
Inspirational Speaker and Life
Coach
Certified Grief Specialist

Chapter 11

MOVE THIS BATTLE FROM MY MIND

By Tynia Canada

"Be not deceived; God is not mocked: for whatsoever a man soweth, so shall he also reap." Galatians 6:7

This recently divorced couple were educated and had very successful careers. They had two children that attended private schools and participated in extracurricular activities. Their eldest child was a senior in high school preparing to attend college out of state. The husband was ordered to pay child support and half of the college tuition. The mother waived her rights to the alimony she was entitled to.

After the eldest child received her college acceptance letters and decided which school she would attend, her parents were expected to pay their portion. The father said he was no longer working and did not pay his share. The father discussed this with his boss, who agreed to say that he was fired and paid him in cash instead. This was because the courts could not trace his income, all to avoid paying child support for his children.

The father gloated at the thought of what he was getting away with until God intervened. You see, he had a praying ex-wife that never wished anything bad in his life. She wanted to live a life that was pleasing to God. Three months later, the husband became very ill, unable to work. His boss told him he could no longer pay him as he wasn't working and gave him six months of severance.

The father was unhappy with the decision; however, he had no other recourse. During his time off, he felt very lonely. His boss stopped calling to check on him, and his friends stopped coming by, which caused him to become depressed. He shared this with his doctor, who told him his health was not improving and he may have to hire an aide to come in a few hours daily to assist him. He also referred him to talk with a psychotherapist.

During one of his sessions, he shared how he regretted the way he treated his children and his ex-wife. He felt that God was punishing him. He asked God for forgiveness and gave three months of severance pay toward his daughters' tuition. The prayers of his ex-wife asked God to show him his unhealthy ways, to be a caring father to their children and for him to develop a personal relationship with God.

She cast her cares in the hands of her God, and he intervened in a way that the father was compelled to reflect on his actions that led to his current situation and a personal relationship with God. This shows us the power of prayer.

My personal story is very similar to the scenario in terms of reaping what you sow. I shall begin by sharing the story of novelist Alice Walker's book "The Color Purple", which turned into a movie.

Focusing on the character Celie, played by actress Whoopi Goldberg, who exemplifies much of what I experienced emotionally throughout some parts of my court battle with my ex. Her biological father abused Celie. Then he married her off to an abusive pimp that abused her even more than her father did. She raised his children and was physically, sexually, mentally and emotionally belittled by him. She was separated from her sister, who lived in Africa and longed to reunite with her. You will learn how her faith in God allowed her to persevere.

My ex was an absent father by choice during the early formation of our son's developmental years. His family adored me and welcomed their first grandchild. They came to the hospital at his birth to welcome his arrival into the world.

My child and I had a beautiful life together, filled with love and security. He was intelligent, had a great sense of humor, and started reading when he was three. My family were very supportive of us, and my mother was phenomenal. I asked her to teach me how to raise my son the way she raised me, and she was elated by my request.

When he was about two years old, his pediatrician inquired how I felt about scheduling him for an intelligence test. As a new mother, I had no idea what to expect. I talked it over with my family and decided to have him tested. His results scored Superior. The psychologist explained that his score means that he is a gifted child. He was recommended to begin accelerated educational programs to challenge his intellect and enhance his exposure to discover other strengths. I was so proud of my baby and thanked God for this blessing.

I began to search schools for gifted children, and we attended interviews with a few schools to see what the best fit was for him. Most of the schools required an assessment and interview for admittance. After carefully searching several schools, we seriously considered The East Manhattan School for Bright and Gifted Children in Manhattan, New York. We scheduled his interview, and he was accepted.

The school had an excellent program, and I watched him thrive at 2 ½. I enjoyed observing him and the other students as they engaged fiercely with complex materials that foster and teach critical thinking skills, leading these gifted students to excel in rapidly accumulating information and facts at an early age. As educators and parents of a gifted child, our children know far more about their choice of interest than we would ever know.

One of my fondest memories is the school's assembly program. The students rehearsed and displayed their knowledge of a variety of subjects. My son was taking private drum lessons from a professional drummer, and I purchased him a drum set. He had his first solo drum performance at the assembly and was cheered by the audience. I had a 45-minute drive to get to work after I took him to school. At times I struggled to ensure he arrived at school on time due to my schedule as a schoolteacher. Later, I was fortunate to get help from another parent who began to take him to school for me, and I later hired a nanny. Yes, I said us because I needed help too.

Our Nanny was resident with us, and she helped tremendously! Her presence allowed me to have more quality time with my son and take him to his extracurricular activities.

After teaching over 30 students in my classroom, preparing lesson plans, and grading papers, I would be exhausted. He was such a joy with a great sense of humor. I smile now as I am sharing this moment with you. During holidays and vacations, we would travel to Virginia Beach, Virginia, to spend time with my parents. He was their youngest grandchild, and he loved to spend time with them.

While he and the Nanny were visiting with his grandparents, I received a letter from an attorney saying that his father wanted to set up regular visits with our son. This surprised me because he knew where we lived, had my phone number and could reach us at any time. His family interacted with us regularly, and he knew this. He never called me once to say that he wanted to see our son. I called and spoke with his family about his complaint, and they said they knew nothing about it.

This marks the beginning of our custody battle.

I had not spoken to his father in about three years. Now, suddenly, he decides to seek counsel to visit our son. He never attempted to call even his parents or me to let them know that he has agreed to see our son after three years.

He never contacted me to ask how he was doing, and he never experienced any of his milestones. His first step, his first tooth, his first cough or anything else. Why now? Did he get an epiphany to develop a father-son relationship after being absent from his life for three years? All these questions were going through my head. My son and I were in a great place in our lives. He was happy in spirit, healthy, auditioning for commercials, and had a lifestyle that afforded him everything that he needed and wanted.

I spoke with my parents about him asking to see our son and the falsities he put in his petition. He was not telling the truth and was fabricating information. I met with the attorney, and he delved into our past. He asked questions such as how we met, how long we'd known each other, our job titles, family history, educational backgrounds, and how we got to this point to get the court involved. He also asked about my son's personality, education, friends, activities, and involvement with family members on both sides. This meeting took about three hours. Afterwards, he said that I needed to give some various times so that he could meet our son again. I could not believe this was happening. He has been absent by choice for all of these years, and now he comes back and demands his time with no regard for our son's feelings. He was allowed to disrupt his life and our lives without remorse or consideration.

A court date was set to answer his petition. His father lied to the courts, saying that he did not know where our son lived, did not have any phone numbers, did not know my workplace, and accused me of "hiding" our son from him. I provided proof that he knew where I worked by a harassing letter he sent to my place of work, threatening me during my pregnancy. I told my principal at the time, and she was highly supportive. His father's accusations were concocted.

The judge set up a supervised visitation schedule. I told the judge that I was very concerned about our son's reaction to meeting a stranger without me and that I would have to be there to make the introduction with ease.

I had to explain to my son that his father wanted to meet and spend time with him. My son asked, "who is he?" and said, "I don't know him". I had to explain it to my son in a way that he would be able to comprehend.

The visits began with my sister or me. She was able to help facilitate due to my work schedule. The staff at a children's protective agency supervised the visits for about two hours. Sometimes they were shorter if our son was tired or ready to leave.

The supervised visits lasted for a few months. All the while, the father was seeking more time with him and requested overnight visits. He eventually sought custody. For what reason is an absent father trying to seek custody of a child living an exceptional life?

.

To give you a bit of history, my ex and I met in college and became best friends. He was a few years ahead of me but did not graduate. After my graduation, we reconnected and began dating. I was a professional songstress recording and traveling and employed as a schoolteacher for the New York City Board of Education. I loved what I did, and he knew my goals' importance to me. When I told him I was pregnant, he was delighted. He said that everything was going to be okay. As time passed, he didn't want me to work. He said I should care for him like some of his friends' partners. I told him no. I had a thriving music career, and I would not stop because I was pregnant. I told him I would not live with him and stop pursuing my goals. Furthermore, our relationship is over if he could not support and respect my decision. He became angry and told me I couldn't live without him, and if I left him, he would make my life miserable!

Throughout my pregnancy, I performed live, recorded and toured with several great musicians. His work kept him traveling many times as a film/record executive.

Never in my life did I expect to have a pregnancy like this. Fortunately, I was blessed to have the support of my loving family and friends to help me through this journey. My goal was to have a happy and healthy baby. I made sure that I surrounded myself with positivity. I traveled, smiled, and lived with joy in my soul every day. My mother told me that whatever I wanted for my unborn child, to keep myself in a place of gratitude and positivity.

Just as Celie was tormented throughout her life, I felt the same. Once the courts became involved in our lives, it was never the same.

Our lives changed for the worse when he came into our lives. He came to steal, devour and destroy. My once jovial, humorous child turned into a child with tears, constantly crying for his mother. The more I complained about the injustices of the court, the more I was told to go away. The courts were significantly biased towards me. The law guardian would sit with his father in court and support his position. She never considered what was in the best interest of our son. During a visit with his father, he was ill and neglected in his care. When I took him to the doctor, they wanted to know why it took so long to seek medical attention. I explained that I had just collected him from his father. The law Guardian blamed me for his illness, and the judge believed her and said nothing to the father.

In the end, I was broken into pieces. As with Celie, the enemy could not break her spirit and destroy her mind. I am happy to say; that I kept my spirit and mind.

This visitation schedule later turned into a full-blown custody battle that gained national media attention in 2020 across various television shows, newspapers, and magazines.

I am so grateful to share this chapter of my upcoming book, expected to be released in January 2023. In my book, you will hear my whole story and learn how I endured some losses but won the battle!

Tyniacanada.com

Wendy Kier

Women's Empowerment Mentor
Trauma Recovery Advocate
Lead Author of the TRIUMPH
OVER TRAUMA book series

Chapter 12

TRAUMA CONSUMED ME

By Wendy Kier

I am no stranger to trauma; it should have been my middle name.

As a child, I didn't have the happiest of upbringings. I was neglected and abandoned by my alcoholic father at just two years old. Taken into the care of Social Services, where I became institutionalized. During this time, I was shoved from pillar to post, with over 30 foster placements and even an adoption breakdown.

I've dealt with child neglect, sexual abuse, abandonment, emotional abuse, rape, homelessness, domestic violence, poverty, addiction, and losing three jobs due to dyslexia discrimination.

The toxicity of this trauma showed up in my beliefs, thoughts, feelings, and emotions and was acted out in my behavior.

What I've learned on my trauma recovery journey in healing and mentoring others, is that we have been talked into, as part of

153

the human collective, to believe that working through trauma is complex and only qualified experts can deal with it. Let me reassure you that this is a myth! This is far from the TRUTH.

Every one of us has the capacity to recover and heal. The reality for me was that I never knew that this was possible because I had bought into the belief that I was damaged. I could only recover with the support of qualified professionals. I was a causality, a victim of the system.

It wasn't until I was in my late 40s that I started to learn that my recovery and healing were in my hands. Once I understood this, it became relatively easy for me to recover and heal deep emotional scars. Even given the amount of hardship I had to endure.

Trauma's toxic emotional impact
I never felt safe, loved, or wanted and learned that I was disposable from a young age. I was never given a break and found myself going from one traumatic event to the next.

I lived most of my life with the devastating consequence of unmanaged and unhealed trauma.

For example:
- Flashbacks, nightmares

- Dissociation of emotions, emotionally numb
- Hopelessness, worry, fear.
- Addicted to work, afraid to speak out, putting others first and sacrificing my well-being, paranoid, constantly fighting my corner and defending myself, overly agreeable
- Sexualized behaviour, desperate to be loved
- I close down when situations are emotionally stressful and become overtired, and have to sleep regardless of where I am
- Highly- motivated leads to burnout.
- Self-harm
- Low self-esteem, low self-worth
- Possessive, jealous, controlling
- No social life or friends, extreme isolation and loneliness, and difficulty establishing and maintaining relationships. When people get close, I cut them off and push them away.
- Hypersensitive, hypervigilant
- Avoiding conflict
- Rage, mood swings, aggression
- Trusting no one
- Extreme shame and guilt
- Always in my head and disconnected from my body.
- Black and white thinking, all or none, right or left.

- Acting out the trauma and putting myself back into situations
- I always have to be one step ahead of everything and everyone.
- Avoid situations and people, isolating myself when I am in a group.
- Fear of being successful in case I would be abused again.

These are all signs and symptoms of unprocessed, unresolved, and unhealed trauma. I am sure you won't be surprised to learn that I eventually ended up with severe anxiety and depression. I became so consumed by fear that I could not leave my bedroom for six months. Terrified to leave, there was no logic at that time, just an overwhelming sense of danger.

Honestly, I've always been depressed because life has been an uphill battle. Medically I've been diagnosed with having a couple of depressive episodes.

What I find strange, though, given everything that I've been through, is that I have never been diagnosed with complex trauma.

The word trauma is a relatively new word in my vocabulary. It is weird, considering I also spent all that time institutionalized in the care system and then spent another 20 years working with young people at risk in Social Services and the voluntary sector. I've also spent 10s of thousands of pounds on my personal development and training.

Trauma denial is an illness

Trauma denial happens on so many levels it's no wonder that people find it challenging to recover and heal. It is denied in wider society, schools, police, doctors, the media, the court system, and employers. But it is also denied by those closest to us, our friends and family.

Another level of complexity to consider is our level of personal denial. We also deny our experience; this is not something we do consciously. It is a human condition the mind designs to keep us safe and out of harm's way. It's how the brain and body process all sorts of trauma by going into denial, so you don't have to feel the pain all over again.

The last thing your brain will want you to do is look at a painful, traumatic event. It does the best thing it knows how to, which is to deny it. It will do this until you are ready to deal with it; while you are still in denial, the damaging effect of trauma will impact some of the decisions you make. You won't be aware of its impact until you notice things consistently going wrong.

Because the mind and body have not processed it properly, it will still play out.

Part of the human ecosystem is designed to protect you from harm at all costs. It does not matter if it is even right or wrong. That's physical and emotional harm, and it will do whatever it can to keep you out of harm's way and danger.

Whether you make a conscious decision or are making decisions at a deep subconscious level, the beliefs created may not be in our best interest because they have been formed out of the fear of trauma. This then gets acted out in our behavior.

A great example of this was when I was asked to speak at the Association of British Psychologists' annual conference in the UK. Public speaking has always made me feel uncomfortable and filled me with dread. I always thought I was not a natural speaker and struggled because of my dyslexia. Little did I know that some of the trauma I endured as a child was why I was not a natural speaker.

I wasn't just nervous like most people; I was terrified of speaking in front of groups. I just had not recognized what was going on, and I thought what I was expanding was just nerves, not extreme fear.

I arrived at the conference the night before my talk. I made a great effort to get there, travelled hundreds of miles, paid for a hotel, and spent time preparing my speech. I knew I felt nervous, but I pushed those feelings to the side and put it down to speaker's nervousness. I have heard many professional speakers say that you will be fine; it is normal.

However, that night after I got into bed. I experienced a severe panic attack; it was one of the worst experiences I've had in my life. I had no idea what was going on. I had just gotten into bed and was ready to fall asleep. Then suddenly, I felt a rush of adrenaline move from my toes to my head. I jumped out of bed; I was panicking for no reason. I could not get my head around what was going on. I felt extreme terror, and I thought I was going mad. I was pacing the room; I couldn't sit down or keep still.

I was in so much emotional distress it was terrifying and all-consuming; I thought I was going mad. I called my partner Steve and spoke with him until my phone ran out of power.

The only way I could feel some level of containment was to get into the bathtub and curl up in the fetal position. I cancelled my talk, and Steve picked me up the following morning. The drive home was just as terrifying; everything seemed dangerous, I still felt an overwhelming sense of fear, but I had no idea why. I didn't understand what was going on.

I arrived home and made an appointment with the doctor; I was told I had depression and was prescribed antidepressants. My ordeal didn't stop there, as I kept having panic attacks. Again, I headed to the bathroom and prayed for the madness to stop. The bathtub became my second home as it felt like the only place I could get a sense of safety. It took me about six months to recover from this one single episode.

In hindsight, I wish I had gotten a second opinion!
At the time, I didn't have the knowledge or insight to know what was playing out. Now I can stand back and make the connection between the trauma of my past and how this has impacted my life in the here and now. I've used the Trauma Recovery Method™ I designed to carefully get under the skin of what's been happening.

I discovered a lot of unhealed trauma. The trauma of being sexually abused by a group of other children in care, meant that I did not like to be in a large group and to speak out. Combine this with the emotional abuse I suffered at the hands of social care staff and through the social services bureaucracy.

My life was put under a microscope by social workers and other professionals. We had endless meetings where my behavior, emotions and life were put under a microscope. The trauma I had experienced at my father's hands and in care had no meaning because the system was normalizing them. I'd lost my voice and learned to live life through the eyes of a traumatized victim.

My subconscious was telling me that this event was too similar to what I had experienced in the past as a child growing up in the care system, so it closed me down and refused to put me in harm's way. This is how powerful unhealed trauma can be and why it's essential to work through it.

I mentioned earlier that "trauma breeds more trauma" this is a great example. For those few hours, I genuinely feared for my life; the event was truly terrifying. As a consequence, I started to avoid similar situations. The truth is that I have never spoken at an in-person event again for fear that I may have a severe panic attack. The thought of going mad and having to take six months off being mentally ill is something I want to avoid at all costs.

I have, however, found a workaround because that is what gifted dyslexics do! I now only speak online, so I can protect my emotional energy and stop myself from becoming emotionally triggered. I love speaking online, so I created my YouTube channel: Living Life Trauma Free.

Trauma's nature

Trauma's nature is to work hard at keeping you out of harm's way. It's how it works at its core and ingrains itself into your identity and personality. It creates an invisible mask you use to protect yourself and hide behind.

This then plays out in your life; it keeps you prisoner, to your past. Your past is not behind you; it is very much in the here and now and not where it needs to be. This unhealthy toxicity is firmly in the driving seat of your life. Unfortunately, it creates a predictable way of doing, being and outcomes.

There is one thing I know for sure, and that is.

Trauma shows up when you least expect

The thing about trauma is that the long-term psychological and damaging emotional effects are so subtle that they often go unnoticed. To the untrained eye, you will miss it because trauma is sneaky as it gets under your skin and engrains itself into your identity and personality. If you don't know what you're looking for and how it plays out.

This is purely an education and knowledge gap, something you haven't learned until now. This is great because it allows you to understand the skills needed to recover and heal. Trauma doesn't need to shape the rest of your life. You can break the trauma cycle and live a life free of the emotional burden you have been carrying.

I guarantee you that if the trauma you experienced has not been healed, then the long-term damaging effects will appear, impacting and interfering with your life. You may not have put your figure on the pulse and have it down as trauma. This, unfortunately, means for many that they will never be able to reach their full potential because their relationship with trauma is dictating their thoughts, feelings, and behaviour and creating predictable outcomes and futures.

> *"It is why people often become so stuck and cannot find a way forward. I believe stress causes more stress, anxiety breeds more anxiety, and trauma creates more trauma."* **W, Kier**

This is its true nature if left unmanaged.

The trick is learning to recognize when trauma is playing out in your life. How is it showing up and getting in your way? Once you discover this, you can regain control of your life.

Become the gatekeeper of your emotional state and change your traumatic memories. This naturally helps you in reducing your level of worry, stress, and anxiety, helping you to build inner strength and resilience, and improving your relationship with yourself and others.

For many, this will start their trauma recovery and healing journey. Trust me; if you are resistant to change and are thinking what a load of rubbish, this is something you should embrace, as it will change your life.

Yolanda Bibbs

Domestic Violence Advocate
Founder / CEO of Divas Against
Domestic Abuse LLC

Chapter 13

THE CYCLE

By Yolanda Bibbs

I always considered myself to be the black sheep of the family in the way that I was unlike my sisters. They were deemed the pretty ones; I, on the other hand, was teased by them, family and some friends about my features; the darkness of my skin, largeness of my eyes, crookedness of my teeth, and the natural kinky texture of my hair. Regarding my appearance, my self-esteem was never high, and to this day, it is still something I sometimes battle with.

It is bewildering how the retention of adolescent teasing never really diminishes, even when you have grown to learn it was just good old-fashion tongue-in-cheek bantering. I learned at an early age that God blessed me with the gift of using my wit, sassiness, and sense of humor as a defense mechanism to ward off tyrant teasers. If I'm making them laugh while making fun of myself, their focus wouldn't be on teasing me, right? Who would have thought, decades later, that we dark-skinned sisters would be encouraged? Hell, even celebrated for embracing our Noir skin and kinky coils! You will come to understand why this cycle is of importance later.

"YOU BLACK, YOU UGLY; I'VE BEEN WITH PLENTY OF OTHER GIRLS THAT LOOK BETTER THAN YOU"! "WHO'S GONNA WANT YOU WITH TWO KIDS"?

These are just a few of derogatory words the father of my first son would utter to taunt me. Ridiculously, I BELIEVED IT and suffered in silence with his false perception of me. Already plagued with low self-esteem, adding in a lack of self-love, it's little wonder how I effortlessly fell victim to his false narrative (See the cycle?).

It took me quite some time to come to the realization and ask myself, "If I was BLACK, UGLY, AND WOULD NOT BE WANTED WITH TWO KIDS, why did he enter into and continue to be in a relationship with me? Become so insanely jealous if other men talked to me, and most importantly, create a child with me?"

Yep, GASLIGHTING AT ITS FINEST!

This was his "GO TO" tactic to manipulate me, which wiped out my self-esteem, furthered my lack of self-love, and gave him COMPLETE control over me! I'm sure you are wondering how I allowed someone to dominate me, keep reading, and you will see the cycle that brought this about.

I witnessed my father physically, emotionally, and verbally abuse my mother and older sister. I thought this was what love looked like until my mother got the nerve to leave... Daddy and Momma are happy and in love, then on any given day, Daddy hits Momma, then my sisters and I hit Daddy to stop him, then all is well until the next episode of "Don't Hit My Momma!" Life became one BIG RE-RUN, usually with me playing the character of "The Mediator" in calming my father down by uttering something sassy or funny enough for him to forget about using my Mom as a human punching bag (See the cycle?).

At the age of five, after one episode, I asked my Mom, "Why do we stay here?" She replied, "I stay because of you kids." Upon hearing her response, I looked up at her with this perplexed look on my face, put my hands on my hips, and stated very matter of fact, "You don't have to stay here with him because of us; you need to leave, he's crazy"! Hearing this from a pre-schooler was more awakening than hearing it from many adults. It played a big part in her finding the courage to leave after my father's final episode, where she awoke to find him standing over her, holding a gun to her head.

Given the wisdom I bestowed on her at such a young age, who knew, fifteen years later, I would be starring in my very own episodes (See the cycle?).

Undergoing constant teasing of my looks from family and friends and now the absence of Fatherly love created a sense that I was never good enough in my mind. In search to find love and acceptance, thinking that would fill the void in my life, I became promiscuous, only to find myself pregnant during my senior year of high school with someone I thought was the love of my life, but ultimately, he took off. This was when most high school girls decided what college to apply to or what dress to wear to Senior prom. Meanwhile, I was warming bottles, changing diapers, battling depression, and suffering lower self-esteem.

Then comes "MR. RIGHT," although he proved not to be "MR. RIGHT." Foolishly, at that time, he was "MR EVERYTHING"! He was tall, had chestnut brown eyes and curly hair, and could sing! The brother was F-I-N-E, and guess what? He didn't want the Captain of the Cheerleader team or the Homecoming Queen; HE WANTED ME and me with a baby…go figure, right? Of course, this raised my self-esteem like gas prices!

Shortly after graduation, YES, I DID GRADUATE, I became pregnant with our son, and he and I starred in what I thought would be loving episodes of our very own sitcom.

I was confident our new roles would be of him leading as Father, Provider and Protector, and me as the doting Mother and Help

Mate, eventually catapulting us down the aisle to roles of Holy Matrimony.

In the beginning, although far from perfect, all started well; however, soon after our first couple of episodes, our pilot flopped as our characters panned out to be him playing the role of a live-in, non-working boyfriend and me as his "Excuse Maker".

I rationalized the controlling signs of burning my clothes if he deemed them inappropriate, limiting the places I could go, the things I could do, or if I got too full of myself, reminding me I was ugly and that he could do better. The most visible sign was his efforts to isolate me from my family and friends, which was especially true concerning my oldest sister, as he never liked her. I believe early on; he detected that in our sitcom turned drama, her recurring character would be played as my "Protector."

It came naturally to her; this had always been her leading role, she once had words with a guy for speaking provocatively about my breasts, as at a young age, I was developed in that area. I understood her experiences in witnessing and being abused by my father, which allowed her to discern abusive characteristics. If allowed, he knew she would influence me; therefore, "Operation Isolation" went into effect. He managed to cause strife after an argument with her led to a scuffle between him and my brother-in-law, resulting in him firing a shot and the bullet landing in the bedroom where my niece lay sound asleep. For most women, that incident would have been the tell-tale sign! Sadly, I justified his actions as he was defending himself. I was naive and unknowingly aiding and abetting his perversity…yes, I stand guilty.

As time went on, the abuse worsened, going from mental and verbal to physical, such as hitting me because he felt I was inappropriately sitting with my legs in view of his guy friend; pushing me out of a moving car, and leaving me stranded by a bridge.

I could go on and on with details of what I endured, but the irony is that it wouldn't be his derogatory remarks, his cheating, or the abuse that would push me to the edge, but him not being present at our son's first birthday party. Of course, being so young, our son would have no memory of who attended; however, still filled with anguish from my first son's father's absenteeism, his non-attendance spoke volumes and broadcast, yet again, another re-run (See the cycle).

On August 13th, 1994, a change sprouted in me, and a revelation bloomed.

I no longer wanted to broadcast these re-runs, I was done starring in DRAMAS, and the REVOLUTION was not going to be televised! After the party and settling the boys in for the evening, I began to cry. The cry turned into praying, begging God to remove me from this toxic situation. After crying and praying for what seemed like hours, I remember feeling empowered, like God had ordained me with courage and dressed me in the battle armor needed to end the relationship. Subsequently, I had no clue about the fight waiting for me.

Weeks passed without a word from him, but this was a recurring re-run as his "DISAPPEARING ACT" was the norm. When he did call, I didn't answer. I focused on myself for the first time during this harrowing relationship. My lack of response was new to him as I had always been so readily available.

Like most abusers, he would rather walk on hot coals than lose control over me and was determined to get it back. Returning home from the gym, I found him waiting on me at home.

We argued, resulting in him physically abusing me. To keep me from calling for help, he slept with a knife in his hand and our son on his chest, just in case I was tempted to try. The next day, due to me not returning her calls, his cousin came over, saw my injuries, said a few choice words to him and managed to get me out of the house into her car. I still can hear him whispering to me, "If you have "Five-O" (referring to the Police) looking for me, I will come back and burn this house down with you in it!"

Once I got to the hospital, they discovered I had a broken nose, busted eardrum, lips, and two black eyes. I was beaten so severely that the ER Doctor called the Police. In the state of Texas, in criminal cases, the District Attorney's office automatically files charges once law enforcement gets involved. I told the officer, "No, he is going to kill me"! He dismissed it and stated, "There will be a warrant for his arrest; we will be looking for him, but if he shows up at your house, dial 911 and leave the phone off the hook".

Upon returning home, the back door remained unlocked. Family and friends were stopping by delivering food, sympathies, and encouragement. Unbeknownst to us, he was waiting in the alley, watching as everyone came and went. I was in the kitchen preparing albuterol for my son's breathing treatment, and I heard the door open;

I didn't look up as I thought it was a family member coming in, then I heard him say, "I told you if you had Five-O looking for me I was going to kill you". When I looked up, I saw him coming toward me. I saw my mother enter the room when she realized it was him. She turned to get her gun; he then ran after her. When he ran after her, I got to the kitchen phone and dialed

911, leaving it off the hook just as the officer had instructed. It's by God's grace that he never noticed.

By this time, it is leading into September 3rd, 1994, Labor Day weekend, to be exact. A weekend for celebrating and recognizing holidays for laborers, resulting in a non-celebratory laboring weekend for us, as we were fighting for our lives. He had managed to get the gun from my mother and begun to hold us hostage.

He moved us all into one room, as we had two phone lines in the house; he made us call our family to tell them he would kill us. He especially wanted to speak to my oldest sister, and the more she would argue with him, the more he would pistol whip and beat my mother and me. There were moments when he would kick my oldest son (2 years old at the time). It became so unbearable that my mother laid on top of my son and told him, "You are going to have to kill me because I can't let you hit him anymore."

The hostage situation turned into a five and half hour standoff with the Port Arthur Texas Police Department and eventually resulted in my two-year-old son being ripped from my arms, held upside down by his ankles, shot in his back, and thrown outside on his head like a bag of garbage. I was standing so close; that I saw fire come from the gun. The bullet nicked his liver, intestines, and kidneys. He had to be flown to the University of Texas Medical Branch, where he remained in a coma for close to a month.

My mother also had her fair share of injuries; outside of my injuries, I suffered a mild concussion and internal trauma from him stomping on my stomach. I was pretty bad off, to the point my middle sister had to feed me, but by the GRACE OF GOD, WE ALL SURVIVED!

My son's father was sentenced to forty years in prison, but due to a legal technicality, he was granted a retrial and only served seven of those forty years. After being released, he met and allegedly killed his then-girlfriend, was arrested, and reportedly hung himself in jail.

As far as my sons and I, shortly after that unforgettable weekend, we moved to Virginia, where I endured more hardships, such as being destitute, homeless, and on welfare. If you can think it, it happened, but that's an entirely different chapter of my story; however, AFTER ALL THE CHAOS I endured, yet again, by the GRACE OF GOD, I was blessed to meet and am now married to the true love of my life, my giving, caring, supportive Husband.

I have a beautiful blended family secure job, but most importantly, I finally BROKE THE CYCLE! In return for God's favor and my passion for helping other victims dealing with abuse, I founded Divas Against Domestic Abuse (DADA) to provide unprejudiced support through the means of motivating, investing in and enhancing the lives of Victims and Survivors of Intimate Partner Violence through faith-based advocacy, education, and community awareness. I hope to use my story to inspire them to redeem their self-worth, become empowered to break the cycle and live abuse-free lives.

divasagainstdomesticabuse@gmail.com

Epilogue

"The most dangerous person in the world is a person who has nothing to lose."

How frequently have you heard this phrase? Every author in this book has provided a description of a dangerous person's behavior. In order to maintain the image they present to the world, abusers frequently carry out their terrible deeds behind closed doors.

Domestic violence/abuse knows no boundaries when it comes to ethnicity, creed, socioeconomic background, religion, gender, or sexual preference. Around the world, this occurs in all cultures.

Domestic violence and abuse has changed from being a global epidemic to a global pandemic within a pandemic. Deaths surged when the world shut down. Victims were no longer able to leave their houses and endured daily violence.

Sadly, a large portion of individuals think that abusers have mental disorders. Not at all! Because they are the closest to the abuser and will be able to help with prosecutions, society should start believing the victims when they ask for assistance rather than doubting them.

There has been abuse in the past, even if it hasn't been reported (e.g., through restraining orders, 911 calls, etc.).

These authors came together with the goal of saving lives by disclosing the specifics of their abuse so that others could self-identify and steer clear of the dangers we encountered. The experiences in this book provide in-depth descriptions of the abuse experienced, the chances for relief missed by law enforcement, and the steps abusers attempted to conceal their abuse from the public.

Everyone who is being abused is aware of it. Every victim, however, has a strong desire to leave. But it has proven challenging to come up with a safety strategy for departure. Most people are unsure of how to get out or where to go. They have children and pets, the shelters are filled, and they lack the money to escape. However, victimization, condemnation, and offensive remarks are aimed at the victims rather than the abusers. At times, remarks that are the most disrespectful are made towards the victims. But few people challenge the abuser's motivation.

As a society, we must start to refrain from posing the question, "Why do you stay?" The abuser needs to be questioned as to "why do they abuse?"

Stop blaming the victim solely for the abuse; as if she or he had left the relationship, the abuse would have stopped. In contrast, victims who attempt to leave an abusive relationship might suffer physical harm or even death in up to 75% of cases. The abuse will not stop if and when the victims leave.

When victims seek assistance, they are expected to respond to the following comments and questions: are you sure you're not exaggerating the situation; that doesn't sound like the person I know; and why would you make such horrible comments about this person? These questions are frequently asked of abusers who are well-known in the community, hold public office, hold positions of leadership in fields such as medicine, law, and information technology, and hold high-ranking positions in the military, law enforcement, and religious organizations. Abusers hold positions in every financial and occupational status.

Others say things like, "She or he didn't treat me that way," or "The way they're being characterized contradicts what I know about them (the abusers)," among other things. Because you are not the target of the abuse, you have not seen the abuse. Dr Jekyll and Mr./Mrs. Hyde are always hiding in plain sight.

Don't ask the questions mentioned above the next time a person approaches you asking for assistance.

By listening, demonstrating empathy, and refusing to seek confirmation from the abuser, you can decide to be different. Consider offering resources like the domestic abuse hotline as a way to help.

In order to support a friend, family member, or coworker, I will never encourage anyone to put themselves in danger. If you suspect abuse, get in touch with your neighborhood authorities.

Analyze the strategies each author employed to free themselves from their abusive relationships using this book as a guide. To help you however they can, their contact information is provided.

We are appreciative that you bought our book, which gave us the opportunity to share our experiences.

Mildred D. Muhammad

Preview of "Scared Silent"

By Mildred D. Muhammad

"Women who have been involved with abusive men often say that their partners started out being exceptionally attentive and romantic. That was certainly true of John when I first met him. It was on a steamy Labor Day in Louisana, and I had the day off from my job as a data processor at the State Department of Labor. What I remember most about that lazy Monday morning, except that it was hot, was that I had nothing special to do and nobody to do it with. I was a naïve twenty-three-year-old, living a sheltered life at home with my mother."

"My life revolved around church and work. I was ready to have my own life, as well as a real relationship. I wanted to meet somebody to love; I wanted to meet somebody who would care about me. That morning, my mother was bustling around the kitchen when I went inside to tell her that I was going to the corner store a couple of blocks away. As always, she reminded me, "Just be careful.""

Available on Amazon and directly from Mildred D. Muhammad

Preview of "I'm Still Standing"

By Mildred D. Muhammad

"Being free of the abuse and fear that John brought into my life, did not mean that I was free from the aftermath of all the events that had occurred. The life that I am living now is not the life I would be living had John been able to kill me. My children would have had to live their lives without their mother."

"Although I had come to accept that John had stopped loving me a long time ago, I had been puzzled as to why he wanted to kill me. His level of hatred was deeper than I ever imagined. It used to hurt me whenever I thought of how much he hated me. He had told me that I had become his enemy. As his enemy, he felt I had to die."

Available on Amazon and directly from Mildred D. Muhammad

About the Book Creator

Mildred D. Muhammad

Mildred D. Muhammad is a Multi-Award-Winning Global Keynote Speaker, International Expert Speaker for the US Dept. of State, Certified Consultant with the US Dept. of Justice/Office for Victims of Crime, Domestic Abuse Survivor, Certified Domestic Violence Advocate. She travels and speaks on a global platform as the ex-wife of the DC Sniper to discuss her life of terror, abuse, and heartbreak, all while promoting Domestic Abuse/Violence Awareness and Prevention.

Mildred's experience has strengthened and expanded the scope of her mission. She is currently working on "In the Midst of Chaos", a trilogy of anthology books. The first book will be released In October 2022.

Mildred's most recent award is being listed in Who's Who in America as the recipient of the Albert Nelson Marquis Lifetime Achievement Award.

Services

Mildred Muhammad is an award-winning global keynote speaker. She is sought by organizations and agencies, worldwide, to share the very intimate details of her experiences with fear, abuse, and frequent victim-blaming. Her experience has strengthened and expanded the scope of her mission.

Simply put, she was a victim who became a survivor and is now a crusader against domestic violence and abuse.

She speaks to a wide range of audiences, including victims and survivors of domestic violence, advocates, law enforcement professionals, therapists, counselors, mental and medical health providers, university and college students, and military personnel, about what it's like to be a victim and survivor of domestic violence "without physical scars" at various conferences, seminars, and workshops.

Her sincerity is as impressive as her unforgettable story of abuse. She discusses the dangers of PTSD (post-traumatic stress disorder) that soldiers face after returning from a war zone, as well as victims who have been diagnosed with PTSD. She is acknowledged and honored for putting her expertise and experience to good use by supporting the Family Advocacy

Program and its goal of educating, promoting, and putting a stop to domestic abuse in military communities.

These are the top 8 reasons to book her for your next event:

- Action Takeaways
- Authenticity
- Compassionate
- Deeply Inspirational
- Direct
- Easy to Work With
- Encouraging
- and Expertise.

Book Mildred for your upcoming event:

Mildred D Muhammad

MY F.O.C.U.S. LLC

Mildred founded My F.O.C.U.S. LLC with the conviction that trauma, in any form, is the root of people's incapacity to properly move forward in their daily lives. My F.O.C.U.S. LLC's goal is to help people identify any obstacles in their personal or professional lives that are getting in the way of their objectives in those areas. This includes business professionals.

Developing emotional intelligence and learning to live in the NOW can help you find the tranquility you seek and assist you in creating the life you desire.

As your inner confidence increases, you'll feel more comfortable making difficult decisions without looking back. While facing your deepest emotions and terrible experiences, you will learn to love yourself. Patience helps you understand yourself better.

- What will you discover about yourself?
- How can you use it to expand your understanding, expertise, and capabilities?

Only you have the power to change the situation. The only person who can save you is you! Being patient is the first step in becoming your own hero.

TRANSFORMATION IS THE KEY!

Book your free 30-minute breakthrough session. And let's get started on your healing!

My F.O.C.U.S LLC

Printed in Great Britain
by Amazon